WARNING SIGNS:

How to Know If Your Partner Is Cheating—
And What To Do About It

WARNING SIGNS:

How to Know If Your Partner Is Cheating—
And What To Do About It

Dawn Ricci and Anthony DeLorenzo
with Ken Baron
and Frank Gunzburg, Ph.D.

life

Guilford, Connecticut
An imprint of The Globe Pequot Press

CONTENTS

DEDICATION

We dedicate "Warning Signs" to the thousands of women and men who have turned to us over the decades to help them discover the truth about their marriage. Though often described as victims of infidelity, they have revealed to us an inner strength and resolve that make them, in our eyes, among the bravest and most valiant individuals we have had the honor of knowing. We hope the knowledge and skills you gain from "Warning Signs" enables you, too, to discover the truth—and in doing so, begin on your own courageous journey to recovery and renewal.

INTRODUCTION:

Congratulations—You're No Longer Clueless

You've opened this book because you fear your relationship might be falling apart. You wouldn't be holding this book in your hands right now if you were confident that your relationship was on solid ground, unthreatened, and healthy. Not perfect, of course—no relationship is—but not in danger. But you're here, about to read *Warning Signs: How to Know If Your Partner Is Cheating—And What To Do About It,* because you sense trouble. Serious trouble.

Now, the suspicions you harbor may be accurate—or for one reason or another, you could be misinterpreting your partner's behavior (he really *could* be slaving away at the office, working all those extra hours). About the only fact you *can* definitely rely on right now is this one: You simply don't have the facts to confirm, one way or the other, what your intuition or gut tells you—that something feels terribly wrong.

More specifically, you lack the investigative skills and necessary tools required to help you assemble the facts that will conclusively prove—or disprove—that infidelity has entered your relationship. And should you discover that an affair has in fact occurred, you probably don't have the resources, skills, and experience to emotionally deal with the stress, anxiety, and despair brought on by being in a relationship racked by infidelity.

But the book you're holding right now can transform your suspicions, your sense of inadequacy, your frustrations, your fears and, yes, your fury into knowledge, confidence, power, and most of all, control. So rather than living in ignorance of the truth and allowing your emotions to overwhelm you, *you* will be the one who controls the situation, who can take positive actions based upon solid information and sound, proven advice from experts in matrimonial investigations and relationship therapy.

We should know, as the two of us have been matrimonial private investigators for a total of over forty-five years. Considering how long we have been investigating cheaters and the thousands of cases we've conducted, you might think that dedicating our entire professional careers to dealing with infidelity might have desensitized us to the plight of our clients. We certainly have seen it all, and then some. But because every case involves an individual, someone we come to know in a most personal way as her life becomes drastically affected by infidelity, it's impossible for us to turn callous, feel indifferent, or become completely inured to our client's problems. In fact just the opposite has occurred: Our clients' situations, their need for help, their vulnerabilities, and ultimately their strength have inspired us to do whatever we can to help them gain control of their lives, their dignity, and their future. That's what led us to create infidelity.com, the Internet's largest website dedicated to giving victims of infidelity the help, information, advice, and community support they desperately need. And we literally wrote the book on how to catch a cheating spouse. So you're holding in your hands not only our experience and know-how but also our commitment to help you through your situation.

Chapters 2 through 8 are dedicated to a particular category of clues, such as work-related signals or changes in routine and appearance. *Warning Signs* will describe more than 100 distinctive signs to look for, each and every one gathered from the thousands of matrimonial investigative cases we have worked on over the last thirty years.

Has infidelity changed much over that period? According to leading experts in the field of infidelity and marriage, 40 percent to 60 percent (or more) of all married men will be unfaithful sometime during their marriage, and up to 40 percent of women will stray as well. Those numbers, shocking as they may sound to you, haven't changed significantly in the last quarter century. But how affairs are conducted *has* changed. Many of the indications of infidelity in *Warning Signs* did not even exist when our private investigation firm opened its doors over three decades ago. In fact, when we first began catching cheating spouses, none of the tools that today makes having an affair easier than ever—email, universal cell phone usage, instant and text messaging, to name just some of the most popular tools provided by technological advances—was even imaginable let alone available on a large scale.

But some things never change. While the clues you might gather, such as cell phone receipts and email files, can certainly help to prove the presence of an affair, the classic clues still most often confirm cheating: patterns of behavior, altering schedules, changes in temperament, which are just a few of the tried-and-true reliable clues that are every bit as useful now as they were in your parents' and your grandparents' generation. But regardless of whether the clues are as new as Blackberries or as classic as the smell of (someone else's) perfume on his dress shirt, you will benefit from the most complete spectrum of clues available to you—organized and explained in understandable language. Each clue is there to help you find one thing: the truth, the *real* truth. And to find it as quickly, as easily, and as conclusively as possible.

Yet, revealing the truth about infidelity doesn't suddenly or magically resolve all the problems with your relationship: The consequences of a partner's cheating can permeate virtually every other aspect of your life. While knowing the truth crucially affects your ability to move forward as well as your ultimate well-being, it is equally important to understand how best to deal with the new realities those life-changing facts can bring to a relationship.

From almost the beginning of our careers as matrimonial investigators, seeking the truth for our clients was often just the beginning of their needs. Once a person's worst fears are confirmed, a whole battery of emotional and relationship issues almost invariably arises. So beyond being one of the most comprehensive presentations of clues to look for if you suspect your partner is cheating, *Warning Signs* also offers you the expert observations and advice of Dr. Frank Gunzburg, a nationally recognized psychologist and author, who has dedicated his professional career to relationship counseling, specializing in helping individuals and couples—the victim and the cheater—work through the trauma of infidelity.

Helping thousands of people who suffer from infidelity has shown us that what they need most is the truth, and afterward the understanding of how to *deal* with the truth. By including professional advice in every chapter to help you cope with the emotional consequences of infidelity, we believe that no matter who you are, or how difficult a situation you're in, *Warning Signs* is going to be one of your greatest allies during this tumultuous time.

How to Rate Your Warning Signs

Warning Signs provides the most comprehensive and thorough compilation of signs to look for in a cheating spouse. But in offering such a complete catalog of clues—from the most furtive and sneakiest to the most arrogantly blatant—to help expose an affair, we also want you to recognize that not every sign is one that applies to your particular situation. Tolstoy observed that "every unhappy family is unhappy in its own way." He easily could have been describing every family shattered by the turmoil of infidelity—as every couple we have dealt with experiences infidelity uniquely in its own way. One of the most common phrases we hear from a client when we refer to other cases similar to her own is, "Yes, that sounds like us, except . . . ," and each time we're reminded of just how individual each situation is, including your own.

So rather than trying to link every warning sign presented on these pages to some action your spouse takes, we recommend a more productive strategy: Give each warning sign a numerical value, from one to ten, using the lower numbers to denote those signs not as relevant to your situation, and higher numbers to identify those signs that seem to more accurately match your partner's behavior and actions. For example, if your spouse has not shown an interest in joining a gym or in losing weight, then assign a low number to those particular clues; on the other hand, if your partner seems to have rather suddenly become more concerned with getting into shape, assign a high number to the clue. The clues with high numbers—and be prepared, there may be quite a few of them—are the ones to concentrate on right now, the ones to follow closely, and, when appropriate, the ones to document (how to document a specific clue is detailed in the description of each clue on the log sheets at the end of Chapters 2 through 7—we also include a blank calendar at the end of Chapters 3, 4, 5, and 7, as well as 12 month-to-month, day-to-day calendars at the back of this book, to help you identify patterns of behavior).

Recognize, of course, that the more cautious a cheating spouse is, the more challenging it will be for you to discern which clues to study. But in our experience, even the cleverest, cagiest, and most careful cheater inevitably leaves a trail of clues that proves infidelity is occurring. And now that you have *Warning Signs* in your arsenal, you're in a far stronger position to find out if your partner is indeed straying. Obviously, you already have your suspicions, or you would not be turning to this book for help. But odd as this may sound, you should approach finding the truth in the most objective, dispassionate manner you can. Try not to read too much into an action—in fact, hard as it might seem, let the benefit of the doubt come into play. This strategy ensures that you won't overreact and tip off your partner that you're on to the deceit, thereby making the truth even more difficult for you to prove. Likewise, overreacting to one or a few clues at the outset of gathering information could make you believe that your partner is cheating when in actuality he is not. We advise our clients to be as methodical and objective as their emotions allow, building the case clue by clue, event by event, over a period of time (usually a few weeks, sometimes longer) until they know without a doubt that their partner is engaged in an illicit relationship.

Another advantage to remaining cool-headed, rational, and systematic during the clue-gathering period is that it will allow you to reflect on the advice of Dr. Gunzburg. And the more informed you are in how to emotionally handle an affair, the better prepared you will be to deal with whatever the truth ultimately reveals.

At the other extreme, don't jump to a conclusion of absolute guilt based on the possibly inconclusive evidence from just one or two signs, such as working late one or two weeks in a row, a couple of unaccountable expenses, or an increase in argumentative behavior. One or two clues generally do not provide irrefutable proof that your mate is in the throes of an illicit relationship. Your partner may very well be having an affair, but it's our experience that one or two signs (other than being caught walking out of a motel room with a lover, or some other overwhelmingly obvious proof) do not constitute convincing proof, signaling that it's time to get the phone number of a divorce attorney. There really is no numerical threshold of signs a suspected partner displays that should be regarded as the tipping point that confirms adultery. Of course, the more signs that align with your mate's actions, the more confident you should feel that your previously unsubstantiated suspicions are indeed based on fact. *Many* facts.

But eventually the evidence points, one way or the other, to the truth. We recommend that you trust your inner voice when trying to determine whether your trust has been broken. When you hear that inner voice say "Enough!" you will know that your instincts were right. We actually call it the "Enough!" moment because it occurs with such regularity with a large portion of our clients. There's no assurance you'll reach your own "Enough!" moment, but you'll find yourself reaching a point in time when you feel confident that your spouse is cheating, based on the overwhelming evidence you have accumulated, warning sign after sign after sign.

How to Read *Warning Signs*

As we've said, no two affairs, no two cheaters are identical. But while each affair is unique, most share basic characteristics. Having caught thousands of cheaters over the years, we've gained expertise in knowing the places to look, the way to look, and the elements to look for—and what to do once we have the compelling evidence that an affair has become part of the marriage equation. We've included virtually everything we've learned in *Warning Signs*. Because of the encyclopedic nature of this book, which places valuable information at your disposal, and your burning desire to know the truth as soon as possible, we realize that you might be tempted to hop from chapter to chapter, from sign to sign, reading a clue here, a sentence there, all to quickly find the signs that most obviously apply in your situation. But please trust us, the best way to read *Warning Signs* is from beginning to end, almost as a narrative. Here's why: Despite the highly sensitive nature of the topic of infidelity, *Warning Signs* should still be regarded as a manual, an instruction book, a guide—and to get the maximum benefit from such a book, it makes sense to follow the instructions from the first step to the last, in an organized, systematic manner.

We've structured the presentation and the order of the clues with two considerations in mind: First, we've ordered the category of clues based on their prominence and frequency. This is why we begin with clues related to your partner's overall behavior and body signals, then his work situation (as work is where most affairs occur), followed by how your spouse is spending money, then moving to other major categories of clues, each valuable but of slightly less frequency (though they certainly could apply in your case). Second, we've coupled the clues with the observations of Dr. Gunzburg, nationally recognized for his work with marriages. He shares his invaluable information in chronological order as the emotions, the events, and the challenges facing an individual or couple unfold when infidelity is first suspected, revealed, confronted, dealt with, and ultimately recedes in dominance, and individuals move on with their life (with or without their partner). So it would not be productive—and could even prompt a premature action on your part—to read the relationship advice in *Warning Signs* out of sequence.

Of course, we do appreciate that it might not be the best way for *you* to navigate this maze of deceit, especially if you're further along in the process of discovering infidelity and dealing with the consequences. If that's your case, then perhaps the à la carte approach to reading *Warning Signs* could work for you—concentrating on those chapters that you know deal with specific signs or relationship advice that meet your needs. This is one reason we made our Contents more detailed than most, so you can easily see the precise topics discussed in each chapter, which should enable those who'd rather concentrate on certain sections to pick and choose.

Hide This Book—and Your Emotions

Keeping *Warning Signs* safely under wraps (quite literally, as you'll soon see) means finding the right time and place to read it, to keep your notes, and to even simply sit alone to mull over what the information in this book fully means to you and your life. We've known clients who keep their notes hidden in their laundry room, under the mattress in the guest bedroom, or at work—though we advise against trying to read our book at the office, as there are too many distractions and, worse, too many opportunities for coworkers to see that your relationship might be in trouble. You should do whatever you can to avoid losing control over who knows what about your relationship, especially the knowledge that it's become a troubled one. If word gets out that you're suspicious, the news could wind up in the wrong hands and ears, such as your partner's.

Chances are your partner is actually too wrapped up in his own deceit to notice what you're reading, but if you think your partner may snoop around, you can easily conceal *Warning Signs*. Simply find a hardcover book on your bookshelf of roughly the same size and try wrapping the dust jacket around this book. It may not fit perfectly, but it will do the trick and help you maintain your privacy. Is this sneaky? Most definitely. But compared to sneaking around to have an illicit affair, the decoy cover hardly even makes a blip on the sneako-meter, does it?

Hiding this book will be the easy part—it will be much more difficult to disguise your emotions during this process, especially when your anger escalates or you feel the acute pain of betrayal. Do your best to follow the advice of Dr. Gunzburg, take care of yourself, and remind yourself that you will have the freedom to fully express your emotions once you have gathered all the facts. Chapter 1 covers some of the essential tools for how to do this successfully so that your own behavior does not arouse your partner's suspicions—and you keep your sanity intact!

You Don't Need a Trench Coat to Be a Super Sleuth

Everything you need for your surveillance is here on the pages of *Warning Signs,* including all the tools required to help you make and maintain organized notes. As you'll see, many clues require that you keep a record of how frequently certain actions occur—such as how often your spouse works late and the specific days of the week those late (or extra-early) hours take place. The goal is to spot a pattern, which often indicates that more is going on than meets your (suspicious) eye.

Keep Cool, Keep Your Eyes Open, and Keep Notes

Always have a pen and paper (or if you have one, your PDA) nearby, because you may need to make an important note while this copy of *Warning Signs* remains hidden away in your linen drawer—or in another safe and secure place. The information on those scraps of paper, in your journal, or however you've recorded the facts, can prove to be invaluable, and you should save it for later when you're piecing everything together.

Thinking like a Sleuth without Acting like One

As we've said, it's critically important that your partner remain unaware of your investigative fact-gathering activities. So besides keeping this book and any loose notes you've made completely out of sight, you also need to keep another item from tipping off your partner that you're on to something. That important item to keep under wraps is *yourself*. You'll do a much more effective job gathering the information you need to determine if your partner is cheating if you act—and this *is* acting—as unsuspecting as possible. Granted, you might deserve the Academy Award for your performance of the ignorant, unsuspecting spouse, and at times you might feel like screaming, crying, slamming a door, or venting through an even more physical way (which is why the next chapter shows you effective methods to control your anger). But your stellar acting performance will be rewarded, not with an Oscar for Best Performance of a Spouse under Duress, but with something far more valuable to you: the *truth*.

How can you possibly act as if you're unsuspecting, unaware, even unconcerned about such things as unexplained expenses, unaccounted-for time away from home, and unaccustomed outbursts from your partner? It won't be easy, and it may even border on the impossible—but you can do it, as we've seen countless wives and husbands successfully handle the role of the oblivious spouse.

One tip is to keep reminding yourself how much your mannerisms, your voice's tone and tenor, and especially your facial expressions and body movements convey how you're really feeling. In fact, in chapter 3, you'll learn how to read *his* most important facial and body language clues to gauge whether he's lying—believe us, your facial expressions and body language convey far more information than you realize. When you're conscious of how you sound and look in your partner's presence and how you react to clues while he's right in front of you, you'll find that you're a natural-born performer. Remember, you're not lying—quite the contrary, because you're working to find the truth.

Another tip is to bear in mind that this is a relatively short-term situation—you're not going to have to pretend (in front of your partner anyway) for an open-ended period that everything is just ducky and hunky-dory when you really know better. We can't predict how long you will have to perform this necessary charade, though it's likely to be a matter of weeks, not months. But when you're under such intense emotional stress, even a matter of weeks can sound like an excruciatingly long time; we know. And Dr. Gunzburg's advice will help you deal with the stresses you'll likely face. After your acting performance begins (in fact, it probably already has, right?), you'll be surprised at how naturally you'll be able to maintain it. Even better, once you've gathered enough clues to prove conclusively and undeniably that your partner has been straying, he or she will be amazed and, yes, humiliated by how well you duped him or her in your pursuit of the truth. That alone should inspire you to put on your acting hat, walk onto the stage, and begin Act I.

Be Precise, Be Complete, Be Brief

We know you're not assembling all these facts about your partner's suspicious actions because you plan on arguing your case in front of the Supreme Court of the United States or in front of any court, as adultery is no longer considered a crime. In some states it is not even grounds for divorce. Almost all states recognize what is known as a "no-fault" divorce based on "irreconcilable differences" or "irremediable breakdown of the marriage." That is, neither party is to blame for the marriage's falling apart. However, there are grounds that are "fault based," and these vary by state. In this latter case, adultery might be a ground, along with other reasons such as drug addiction and abuse, among others. If you do plan to file for divorce, we suggest you discuss with a divorce attorney whether or not adultery can or should be a part of your divorce petition. The reality is that you need to prove this first to the two people to whom facing the truth about this affair matters the most—yourself and your partner.

When confronted with the indisputable truth that a suspecting spouse (and perhaps a private investigator) discovers and documents, most cheating partners will have little choice but to admit to their adultery. But each infidelity is different, and while there's no way to predict how your partner will respond, the more evidence you have the more likely an admission of wrongdoing will be made. The admission—or, if you prefer, confession—might not be immediate. But with enough evidence, most adulterers do admit that they have cheated. The key, of course, is in making sure your case is as solid as you can make it.

To ensure that you gather enough compelling proof, you need to monitor your partner's actions, attitude, and activities as closely as you can without raising your partner's suspicions that you're sleuthing. Not an easy task, and right now you might regard this as next to impossible to pull off effectively. But in helping thousands of wives and husbands whose suspicions needed confirmation, we've seen that the practical need to act unsuspecting trumps the emotional need to just let loose and exclaim, "I *know* what's going on!"

The entries you make in your journal need to have only the barest of information, such as date, time of day, and whatever other information the appropriate log sheets and calendars in *Warning Signs* require You don't need to editorialize or turn these sleuthing log sheets and calendars into your diary or memory book—you can keep a separate journal for your emotions if you need one, and Dr. Gunzburg has many worthwhile suggestions on how to do that (see pp. 41–46). Your job—and it will help you to indeed regard this activity as a job—is to collect facts, pure and simple. "Just the facts, Ma'am, just the facts," as the taciturn detective Joe Friday would request on the famous television show *Dragnet*.

Six Tips for Remaining Calm and Collected

As you can imagine, over the years our private investigation firm has conducted tens of thousands of surveillance operations in pursuit of catching cheating spouses. Often in these cases, we need the assistance of our clients to collect information that will help us in our undercover work, which means the suspecting spouse must be, by extension, an undercover agent of sorts. And by working with so many wives and husbands, boyfriends and girlfriends, and even other family members in catching a cheating family member, we've learned what it takes for a nonprofessional like yourself to become a successful sleuth, if only temporarily. The minute you begin to gather information and look for signs that your partner is cheating, you'll see that the advice you've just read in this chapter will be immensely helpful to you.

But despite what you've learned here, none of it will matter if you cannot remain focused, calm, and in control. To that end, here are six vitally important tips that we make sure to give to all our clients before they begin and that they can keep referring to while gathering each and every sign. Repeat to yourself the following:

1. *This is a project, a job, maybe the most important job I'll ever have.* I don't see it as a burden, or distasteful, or possibly pointless. It is, simply, one of the most important activities I'll ever be engaged in.

2. *This is a brief, temporary job, one that's going to last only a few weeks.* It will be over sooner than later, and I'll never have to do this again.

3. *The less my spouse suspects that I'm doing this, the greater my odds of finding out the truth.* So I can't let on, I just can't let on what I'm doing.

4. *My spouse is putting on a great, big act—why shouldn't I?* This is not a version of two wrongs don't

make a right. The fact is a wrong act demands that I react by using the best tools and methods at my disposal.

5. *I'm going to be a better actor than I think (and, later: I am a better actor than I ever thought I could be).* And I should be prepared for the fact that he's a fine performer as well.

6. *I will make it a point to have a "cool-off" contact.* (This should be a good friend, a close relative, or a therapist you can call if you think you're about to lose your cool. Don't feel awkward about needing this person when you're about to snap and possibly let your partner know that you know something is wrong. Call your cool-off contact when you abso-lutely have no other way to calm yourself down—and by all means call rather than risk blowing your top, and as a consequence blowing your cover as a sleuth. Also, in chapter 2, Dr. Gunzburg shows you how to cope with the initial trauma.)

Be Your Own Sleuth

You have *Warning Signs* in front of you because you're dedi-cated to finding the truth about a possible affair. And that's what you will find, one way or the other. Every warning sign in this book derives from our decades of experience investigating thousands of matrimonial cases. You *will* learn the warning signs that indicate cheating is indeed a high probability and possibly an absolute fact. But just as important as what those warning signs are is the fact that you need to assume *our* role, the role of a sleuth, to gather, identify, and use those signals to confront the cheater with the truth. We suggest you review this chapter from time to time, to make sure your sleuthing skills are fully engaged, paying special attention to keeping cool in the face of revealing the most damning and hurtful facts. In the next chapter, we'll help you to recognize some of the most obvious signals or signs of infidelity.

CHAPTER 2

The Signals of Change

Because we have been matrimonial private investigators for decades you'd think that we've seen it all, especially when it comes to how cheaters try to keep from getting caught. But the reality is that we continue to be astonished at the elaborate, almost ingenious, deceptions that cheaters employ to make sure—usually in vain—that their affairs remain a secret.

Some cheaters seem to dedicate more time to hiding their affairs than they spend with their cheating partner. One client's husband created fake, detailed office memos to show to his wife that were supposedly sent from a boss requesting that the husband work on the weekend—of course he spent the entire day not at his desk but in a motel with his lover. Another cheater we investigated created bogus email accounts from fictitious clients who would request meetings in the evenings. The cheater would forward the emails to his wife, apologizing for having to be out late. The clients didn't exist but the girlfriend did.

Imagine if cheaters like these could use the same level of ingenuity and energy on worthwhile activities and not on deceiving their wives. Who knows, they might receive a promotion at work, earn a patent, or write a great screenplay. Instead, their energies are focused on scheming, deceptions, and creating decoys, all designed to hide their illicit behavior. But no matter how diligently cheaters labor to construct their tangled web of deceit, they are likely—and unwittingly—displaying high-level warning signs in the form of changes in behavior. These "Change Signals" might not be equivalent to wearing a placard reading "I'm a cheater!" but they are almost as obvious as that *if* you know what Change Signals to observe. In this chapter, you'll learn all the most important ones; some may be occurring in your home right now though unrecognized as yet, others you've likely already noticed, and still more will make an appearance in the near future. But take note of them all, even those that you feel don't apply to you, because when it comes to having an affair, *anything* is possible.

In Nathaniel Hawthorne's great novel *The Scarlet Letter,* a woman accused of adultery is forced to wear the letter A embroidered on the bodice of her dress, an emblem constantly reminding the entire community that she committed the sin of adultery. If it were only that easy to spot an adulterous spouse today. But even though cheaters don't wear a placard reading "I'm a cheater" or a scarlet letter A, we do tell our clients to use the letter A when seeking clues at home that a spouse's heart is someplace else. That's A as in Appearance, Actions, and Attitude. Granted, these words don't wield the accusatory weight that the original scarlet letter does, but the Change Signals of Appearance, Actions, and Attitude still can prove to be almost as accurate in fingering an adulterer.

Change Signals—When the Same Old Same Old Doesn't Hold

Most of us, as creatures of habit, adhere to our own daily regimen; we continue to enjoy our favorite foods and music or take the same kind of vacation year after year. We are who we are, and much of who we are is made up of our consistent habits, patterns, and preferences. Of course, we may change jobs, move to a different locale, add a few pounds, or turn a bit grayer, but our basic makeup—our personality, our core beliefs, our way of dressing—all remain pretty much the same over time.

This practice of sticking to routine behavior, repeating patterns, and keeping habits helps us to maintain a sense of order and control in our lives. "Oh, that's just like him," "I knew you'd enjoy this," and "It was made just for her" are expressions we've all used. These expressions testify to the universality of our inclination to act in consistent, predictable, expected ways. Of course, we're not programmed robots or trained circus animals—we're humans who every so often veer away, sometimes far away, from our predictable behavior, which is also a very human trait. Often, external forces and events inspire those changes in habit, such as a visit to a doctor's office where we're admonished to lose weight, get in shape, take up new activities, and eat more healthfully. Vanity, as well, is an equally powerful motivator that we humans share. The impulse to look as good as possible is a natural characteristic most of us have to a greater or lesser degree. And endless marketing campaigns stressing the value of looking our best nurture this impulse. If a man decides that he wants to tone down his ever-encroaching gray with a hair color treatment, it's foolish and presumptuous to assume that the reason he's trying to look younger is to be more attractive to a younger woman he's hoping to seduce. Most likely, he's merely making changes to feel better about himself, especially in a culture that prizes a youthful appearance.

But there are other changes people make that aren't so innocent or banal. An affair is based upon an entirely different dynamic about change, one that prompts the cheater to alter the way he presents himself, how he feels about sex, his interests, and what he wants in life. These changes might be subtler or harder to detect than coloring his hair. But if you know how and where to look, they'll be as obvious as that new form-fitting shirt he's taken to wearing. The irony is that as fanatically careful as a cheater can be in hiding his affair from his partner, family, friends, and work associates—with secret hideaways reached by roundabout routes to avoid being seen, for example—his other actions blatantly betray the betrayal. Most cheaters do not appreciate that mere changes in Appearance, Actions, and Attitude are an open admission of having an affair. Yet these Change Signals often reveal the scarlet letter A for adulterer.

Of course, some cheaters (although rare to the species) do not display one single Change Signal introduced in this chapter. But it is unlikely you'll experience the phenomenon of a cheater who is able to conduct an affair without changing, literally, a hair on his head or buying a new shirt or visiting a gym or displaying at least several key elements that often though not always should be regarded as possible warning signs of an affair.

As with other large and small warning signs a cheating spouse might display, do not react by immediately and vociferously demanding an explanation. Not only will there be ample time to confront him, but you'll likely have a more comprehensive and conclusive arsenal of evidence of his cheating if you wait a bit longer. Another reason not to reflexively challenge him on one or another Change Signal he's displaying is because there's a small chance that a particular change or set of changes has nothing to do with his having an affair. So we strongly suggest that you don't point an accusatory finger until you have a host of indisputable evidence in hand, which you most certainly will.

Not all Change Signals are created equal. Some are apparent to the whole world, and others are more intimate so only *you* would know about the change. But almost all of them have a few things in common, the most obvious of course being the fact that many of the changes would not occur if there had not been an affair. Another quality most of the changes share is how intensely personal the changes in his behavior are— changes dealing with appearance, personal preferences, ways of relating to family and friends. And, for the most part, you'll likely notice that most of the changes you observe began more or less at the same time.

So the hallmarks of Change Signals are

- they cover a *full spectrum* of changes.
- they are *consequences* of an affair, not the *cause* of it.
- they are *personal* changes in *Appearance, Actions,* and *Attitude*.
- they more or less *arise at the same time*.

Your spouse probably won't display all the Change Signals in Appearance, Actions, and Attitude (though we've seen some who come remarkably close). But chances are you will identify a number of changes that do match his altered behavior. Knowing which changes apply to your particular case is rather straightforward, as the changes are self-evident. Change Signals alone should not be interpreted as conclusive, positive proof that you've been cheated on. When added to the other signs you uncover with the help of *Warning Signs,* you will have assembled enough facts to give you the confidence of knowing that when you do confront him with the charge of having an affair, you'll be armed with ample, even overwhelming, evidence not just suspicions.

Appearance—Change Signal Number One: He's Got That Look of Love

No, you can't judge a book by its cover, and you can't judge people simply by how they look. But when a spouse begins to alter his appearance in numerous ways, unaccompanied by any stated or believable motive, then take serious notice. If any single aspect of cheaters is universal it's this: The affair can inspire a cheater to reinvent his appearance, literally from head (getting rid of that gray) to toe (new shoes, along with new shirts, a whole new wardrobe).

Suddenly a Clotheshorse Rides into Town

I used to get his shirts at places like Sears and Walmart. Suddenly, he's buying $60 sports shirts at a fancy men's store!

He never even asked for nice shirts as gifts; he only wanted to wear the basic button-down shirts to the office and more casual ones on the weekend. Then, starting maybe a couple months ago, he's been the one buying his own shirts, a new shirt every other week, one fancier and more form-fitting than the next. Same with the pants he's wearing, now they're pleated, and not just black or brown either. He says he's wearing nicer clothes to look better in the office. But I knew it had to be something more, a lot more. And I was right.

—*Lucille R.*

Most of us like to shop for—or receive—new apparel, especially when the seasons change. But what you should be sensitive to is a spouse's abrupt interest in clothes accompanied by a concern over how he thinks he looks in the new clothing. Your partner's clothes closet can hold the first, and in many cases, the most obvious signs that an affair is in the making or actually going on. If he never had a reputation as a clotheshorse but has recently started displaying an interest in clothing, it could be a sign that he is trying to impress a lover (or soon-to-be lover). So that sexy new look your spouse is sporting might not be meant for your eyes.

With many couples, especially those who've been together a good while, the wife either buys most of her husband's clothes or at the least is very influential in what he decides to purchase. Of course, this might not be the case with you at all, but for millions of women, a new shirt in a husband's closet is usually a result of the wife's buying it for him or at least being with him when he bought it.

This pattern can change dramatically when the husband is having an affair. His button-down oxford shirts get pushed to the back of the closet, replaced by a half dozen new, brightly colored shirts. The cheater wants to appear as young as possible in the eyes of his lover, so the new clothes he buys are often designed for men half his age. If the new clothes making a debut in his closet are age appropriate, they may be far more expensive than the regular cotton dress shirts he usually wears. Feeling fit and sexy because of the affair, a cheater might be more inclined to spend hundreds of dollars on tailor-made clothing, all to impress his lover. But you should be suspicious, even if the clothing purchases are of far less value than custom clothing, if the new items are much more fashionable or more daring than what he traditionally wears, if they are worn on days that you also suspect he is seeing his lover, and, though not as expensive as tailor-made clothing, if the new clothes are far costlier than what he (or you) usually spend on his clothing.

Also, be aware that some of his new clothes "purchases" are actually gifts from his lover. Lovers often exchange gifts of apparel or fashion accessories; these items serve as symbols of affection and another way to maintain their closeness when they are apart. If your spouse suddenly sports an expensive new fashion item and you're unsure of its origin, review charge card receipts (see chapter 5, pp. 111–15) to find out if he bought it or received it as a gift. Don't ask him about the item outright; you don't want to tip him off to your suspicions until you have other pieces of evidence at your disposal.

Women having affairs often begin to wear sexier, more revealing apparel. So a woman who begins showing more cleavage than usual can actually be revealing her desire to look even sexier to her lover. And the clothes you're not supposed to see can also be an important clue of infidelity—finding her new lingerie or his sexy men's briefs hidden away in an attaché case or exercise bag is likely evidence of a spouse's secret double life.

The Clues	The Meaning
• New style of clothing	• Feel sexier in the eyes of the lover
• New-found interest in clothes	• Clothes impress the lover
• Wearing more expensive clothes than usual	• Could be a gift from the lover; wants to impress the lover

Only His Hairdresser—and His Lover—Knows for Sure

He used to joke about other guys coloring their hair. And now look at him, Mr. Brunet.

My cousin colored his hair, and Bill couldn't stop making fun of him, calling him the Clairol Kid. And Bill already had a full head of gray hair, which I always thought made him look distinguished. About a month ago, I noticed that his hair was getting darker, but I thought no, he couldn't possibly be coloring it, not my Bill. But I looked in his bathroom cabinet, and there's the bottle of Just for Men. When I asked him, in the nicest way possible, why he hadn't told me he was darkening his hair, he barked back that it was his business, all the guys were doing it. Him being so defensive made me even more suspicious.

Anne T.

Thanks to marketing successes like Grecian Formula, Just for Men, and other brands of men's hair-coloring products, much of the stigma associated with a man's tinting or coloring his hair has vanished along with the gray hair. Of course in a society that prizes a youthful appearance as much as we do, it certainly isn't surprising that so many men have lost their gray (except for that stylish touch of gray at the temples). But if you suspect your husband is cheating, there may very well be another motivator for coloring his hair than simply taking a few years off his appearance—it might also be because he wants to look as young as possible to his lover (whom he might have lied to about his age). So while coloring one's hair is common and accepted, if your husband begins doing it in conjunction with other Change Signals you've identified, it should be regarded not just as normal vanity but as a possible sign of cheating. The same can be said for a new hairstyle, especially a style worn by much younger men. Again, the motivation could likely be to appear younger to the world at large (and to himself), but it could also be a sign that he wants his lover to see him as a much younger man. But color and cut aren't the only ways his hair can give you clues to possible infidelity. Some women love mustaches and beards, while others dislike them. If your partner either starts growing a mustache or beard, or has been bearded for years and suddenly one morning shaves it off, and this occurs in combination with other signs, it may have been motivated by the lover's suggestion.

The Clues	The Meaning
• Colors his hair	• Looks younger to his lover
• New hair style	• Wants to appear hipper, cooler
• Grows or shaves a moustache	• Request of his lover

Mirror, Mirror on the Wall, Is He Cheating?

He spends more time in front of the mirror than I do!

One of the things I loved most about our new house was that the master bathroom had two sinks with two big mirrors. I remember Jimmy cracking to friends that I'd be in heaven with two mirrors all to myself since he needs a mirror just for his quick shave in the morning. Well, surprise, surprise. Just in these past couple of months, Jimmy's filled his cabinet with creams and bronzers and tonics—really expensive ones, too. And it's a good thing we have those two mirrors, or else

I'd never have a chance to put on lipstick in the morning because it seems like Jimmy spends more time in front of the mirror than I do. I never used to think that my husband was vain, but there's no other word for it. Now I'm thinking other thoughts too.

Beatrice E.

When you live with someone, that person's habits, mannerisms, and disposition become as familiar to you as your own—he doesn't like the seeds in tomatoes, she sleeps with two pillows, he flosses first then brushes and she's the opposite. So you probably know his grooming patterns as well as he does. You've seen him splash on aftershave and comb his hair so many times, you should be able to describe the order and the length of his grooming activities down to the last swig of mouthwash before he walks out of the bathroom and off to work. Now you can use that knowledge to determine if he is possibly having an affair. Pay more attention to his procedures and notice if he's spending additional time getting ready, adding other elements to his daily grooming such as skin creams, bronzers, more expensive and elaborate hair conditioning treatments, and, of course, new brands of cologne as well as wearing more cologne. An increased devotion to grooming that coincides with other Change Signals means that while he might be looking better, your relationship might not be.

Now, most of us display a certain amount of vanity, and there's nothing wrong with that—we all want to look good to the rest of the world. But you should take careful note if your spouse becomes increasingly involved with his grooming, especially when getting ready to go to the office (where the lover might also work). If out of the blue and without discussing it with you first, your spouse announces that he is getting his teeth whitened or is seeing a doctor for Botox injections, you should consider such actions as possible signs that he is attempting to look younger and more attractive for his lover—and, unfortunately, not for you. Use the Major Change Signals chart on p. 49 to keep track of any increase in grooming and grooming products.

The Clues	The Meaning
• Sudden increase in grooming time	• He wants to look his best for the lover
• Wearing new perfume or cologne	• Possibly a gift from the lover, as it could be the lover's favorite scent
• New hair color or makeup techniques	• Attempt to look sexier to the lover

I Can See Clearly Now . . . That You've Been Straying

He'd criticize me for spending too much for nice frames, and then comes home wearing a pair of Ralph Lauren glasses that must've cost him $400.

The kids used to joke about David's aviator eyeglass frames, saying they made him look like someone in a seventies spy movie. And he never cared, because he thought glasses are just glasses and spending more than $50 for frames was nuts. I still can't get used to his new ones, like something a male model a third his age would be wearing. Why would someone so clueless about fashion even bother? That question made me start thinking about all the other things that were changing.

Rebecca S.

About fifteen years ago, we began to notice that more and more of our clients commented on their cheating spouses' having bought new eyeglasses within the last few months (this would occur about the same time that the wives began suspecting infidelity). Many would say they were surprised at the frame choice made by their husband, which was invariably more "fashion forward" than the husband's previous pair of eyeglasses. This increase in clients' reporting about their husbands' new eyeglasses appeared around the same time that sales of designer eyeglass frames skyrocketed. And no wonder, for now a consumer could make a fashion statement by donning a pair of Ralph Lauren, Calvin Klein, or Armani eyeglass frames. It didn't take great insight to make the connection between expensive, fashionable eyeglass frames and signs of a cheater trying to look his best for his lover.

Along with the appearance of a new pair of Italian-style eyeglasses as a possible warning sign comes the possible disappearance of his eyeglasses altogether. If your partner announces that he no longer wants to wear eyeglasses and is getting examined for contact lenses or even is submitting to costly Lasik surgery, a warning bell should go off—especially when you add it to a number of other Change Signals he's displaying.

The Clues	The Meaning
• New, expensive eyeglass frames	• He wants to look fashionable, with-it
• Gets contact lenses or Lasik surgery	• Thinks eyeglasses make him look too old in his lover's eyes

Whiten This, Darken That

The dentist's office called to confirm his teeth-whitening appointment, which was surprising news to me.

First, I thought, hey, they're calling for the wrong Jason, 'cause I never, ever thought he'd give a second thought to doing something like that, something so expensive and just for his looks. But then I said to myself, you know, he's bought these news shirts, and now goes to this hair salon instead of the same barber he's had for years. Something, a bunch of things, aren't the same about him.

Judith M.

Purveyors of new products and technologies exploiting our vanity have a ready-made market when it comes to cheaters, the teeth-whitening and artificial tanning categories being among the cheater's most popular choices. Either through do-it-yourself teeth-whitening kits or the far more expensive whitening procedures performed in dental offices, more and more of us are using this popular, easy tool to enhance our appearance. So while turning dull or discolored teeth into sparkling white ones is common, you should still consider it a possible sign of your partner's wanting to look as young, healthy, and fit as possible for his lover—and that's nothing to smile about.

Tanning salons, while not nearly as popular and inexpensive as store-bought teeth-whitening kits, offer another easy way to look younger. In our experience, tanning salon customers are predominantly female, and most of those are younger females. So if you're beginning to notice that your spouse is looking more and more bronzed, and you hadn't yet taken that vacation to the beach, the most logical explanation is that he's been getting those UVs indoors, at the tanning salon. He might opt for self-tanning creams or bronzers, which are safer—but that's still a dangerous signal for you, as he's likely doing it to look sexy and youthful in the eyes of his lover.

The Clues	The Meaning
• Whitens teeth, either with at-home product or at dentist's office	• A younger, more healthful appearance to please his lover
• Visiting a tanning salon or wearing bronzer or self-tanning lotion	• To look more fit and virile for his lover

Action—Change Signal Number Two: Watch What He Does, Not Just What He Says

Even if your husband is a man of few words, or these days fewer and fewer *honest* words, he still could be communicating the fact that he's having an affair, though of course he won't realize that he's admitting it to you. All you need to do is become an astute observer of certain actions and activities, especially when they are new ones. The following are some of the most common actions we tell our clients to take special note of, activities that can tell you something is up without his even saying a word.

Getting in Shape for All the Wrong Reasons

I couldn't even get him to take a walk after dinner for a little exercise, and now he's working out at that gym three, four days a week.

A woman should be happy that her husband has finally decided to get rid of his spare tire and go get himself in shape. And at first I was as glad as I was surprised that Howard joined that gym and has really stuck with it, something I wish I could do. But I'm thinking that the fear of having a heart attack isn't his big motivator here. The new Howard is more than Howard-the-gym-goer; it's also his new clothes, it's growing that mustache I still can't get used to, and it's why I'm thinking what I'm thinking now about him.

Beth D.

There's no question that too many of us need to get in better shape, drop a few (or more) pounds, start an exercise regimen, and eat more healthfully. When a person undertakes such wholesome and worthwhile activities, he should be applauded for his dedication to self-improvement. But let's not be too quick with the compliments if his new membership to Gold's Gym happens to coincide with your deepening suspicions about an affair. Some of the married men and women raising their heart levels on the treadmill machines and lifting weights to be more toned and fit are doing all this not to impress their spouse, doctor, or friends. Instead, all those hours on the elliptical and reps of bench presses are to have a toned and fit body for their lover to admire.

When a person who hasn't worked out in years and has shown little interest in getting in shape suddenly joins a gym, is starting to jog, or is pursuing a similar fitness program, your warning-signs antenna needs to go up. Of course, not every new member of the gym or novice jogger trudging on the side of the road is drawn to these activities because of an affair. But if you talked with spouses whose partners were cheating, as we do every day, you would soon recognize just how prevalent the desire of cheaters is—especially those just beginning an affair—to get into shape.

The Clues	The Meaning
• Joins a gym, after years of not exercising regularly • Obsessed with looking fit	• Wants to get his body looking younger and more toned, to impress the lover

Decreasing Weight Should Raise Your Warning Signs Flag

Maybe everyone cares about their weight. But that's all she cares about.

Julie never was heavy, but after our kid was born, she had a hard time losing the extra weight, then put on a few more pounds, you know, it happens with just about everyone. I never once said anything to her, because I figured what's ten or fifteen pounds anyway, and she always looked great to me. She'd moan when summer came around, "Got to lose these hips," and even if she dropped a few pounds, they'd come back, no big deal. Then maybe four or five months ago, like overnight, she becomes the Diet Dictator; we can't eat out, she joins one of those diet centers, and as far as she's concerned, I'm on my own, foodwise.

Yeah, Julie looks like she did twenty years ago, but it makes me wonder why now, why so fanatical, and why not act like she's doing it even a little bit to make me happy?

Michael W.

It's hard to escape hearing advice to eat more healthfully and to exercise, doctors remind us of the benefits as do journalists and celebrities; even your concerned family and friends join the chorus. Those who do manage to eat well, keep their weight in check, and exercise with some regularity are models for all of us. But when a spouse suddenly throws himself or herself into a demanding diet and exercise regimen, it should raise a warning flag in your mind. While you should want your partner to be in the best physical health possible, you should be able to distinguish between someone wanting to be in decent shape and someone who only recently has become obsessed with looking as buff, trim, and fit as possible.

So along with a cheater's desire to tone, shape, and strengthen his body is often a newfound commitment to dropping a few or more pounds. The reason is obvious: He wants to lose his paunches and flab to look better for his lover. Dieting is about as common today as any activity (it seems like every other person you know is on a diet)—yet as common as dieting is among the population at large, from our vantage point it's even more common among cheaters. If your partner declares that he's finally going on that diet and appears far more dedicated to achieving his goals and maintaining the lower weight, *and* you've logged a growing number of Change Signals and other Warning Signs, then beware: That weight-loss program could mean that while he's lost a few pounds, you have good reason to lose even more trust—because such sudden conversions to getting in shape are often inspired not by what the doctor said but by what a cheating spouse hopes will please the lover.

The Clues	The Meaning
• Sudden obsession about weight and weight loss	• The spouse is trying to appear more youthful and sexy to her lover

Ironically, Sex May Increase

He's never, ever been more interested in sex with me than right now.

I can't put a date on it, but over the last maybe two or three months our sex lives have been more like I remember them when Steven and I were first married. But it's different now, not with the passion and the love all mixed together, more just passion, especially on his side. I'm not always in the mood, but Steven is, especially if he comes home after having a few drinks with the guys. If I don't feel like it, he won't persist, but I can sense he's not happy about it. And even though he's much more easily aroused now than just a while ago, he's not any more loving, maybe even less so. You'd think being married to a guy who likes having sex is good for a marriage, but something about this has been telling me this isn't about me and Steven, it's about something else that's going on.

Charlotta J.

A heightened desire for sex on the part of the suspected cheater remains one of the most common and consistent signs of an affair.

If the cheating spouse is having sex, and possibly passionate sex, with another person, why would his need for sex increase at home of all places? As counterintuitive as the increase in his sexual desire at home might at first seem, it does make sense, although a most peculiar kind of sense. Many cheaters later admit that they encourage more sex as a decoy of sorts, to make the suspecting or unsuspecting spouse feel as if the relationship were untroubled or not under attack. But in this case it's the cheating spouse's overzealous lovemaking that you should question. Another explanation of the possible increase in sex is the overall heightened desire for sex that an affair can engender, at least for a while. An unfortunate corollary of this is the almost perverse excitement that some cheaters experience by sleeping with the spouse they are cheating on.

When a couple does experience more lovemaking as a side effect of infidelity, diminished affection usually also surfaces at these intimate times. This isn't surprising considering the context in which the lovemaking occurs. Because of the lack of intimacy during lovemaking with the cheating spouse, many of our clients express the desire to avoid sex. But until conclusive evidence can be collected, we recommend that the suspecting partner not do anything out of the ordinary that would give the cheater a clue that his affair is already being considered and investigated.

The Clues	The Meaning
• Marked increase of sex	• Possibly a decoy to make you feel nothing is wrong
• Seems to enjoy sex more	• Affair could heighten his sex drive
• Less affectionate during sex	• Thinking of his lover, not where he is

New Sexual Techniques, Often Accompanied with Sex Toys

I was almost afraid to ask him, "So, where'd you learn that?"

This is what happened. Last week, Sid comes home really late for him, was out with some sales guys he says, and it's easy to tell he had had a few, maybe more than a few. I didn't mind that he wanted to have sex, just hoped it wasn't inspired by the booze. As we start, Sid suggests we try something new, this new position he read about. "Read about where?" I ask him, and he can't remember and gets a little uppity that I'm asking. So we try it, no big deal, but he wants to show me another one and by then I'm not going to quiz him, but I am asking myself, "Where'd Sid learn these things?" I just knew he had firsthand instructions. That night, right there and then, I vowed I would learn the answer, no matter what the consequences.

Dianne M.

Infidelity can affect a marriage's sexual component in a variety of ways, covering a spectrum of sexual changes among our clients. At one end are couples whose sexual intimacy has become virtually nonexistent because of an affair; at the other end, spouses of cheaters report that their mate displays a new and heightened interest in sex. Often the increase in sex—say from two or three times a week to four, five, or six—is accompanied by the cheating spouse's introducing and encouraging new lovemaking techniques, sex toys, and enhancements. There was a time not too long ago when we would tell clients categorically that the suspected spouse learned the new techniques and discovered sex toys from the lover. The truth now could be more complicated than that, as it takes just a few keystrokes to find Internet sites displaying all varieties of sexual activities and techniques as well as online stores selling sex toys and enhancements. So, yes, an increased appetite for sex coupled with the introduction of novel ways (novel to you, anyway) to make love, including sex toys and the like can be a product of your partner's surfing the seamy side of the Web. As troubling as that might sound to you, it's still better than his learning these things by firsthand experience. And the fact is, even today when a client tells us her sex life has increased and become more varied, we still almost always discover that the source of this change in the bedroom is because her husband is spending time in another bedroom.

The Clue	The Meaning
• New sexual positions, techniques, and toys	• The new lover has introduced these to your spouse; your spouse wants to continue their use at home to be reminded of the lover

The Lost Weekend

Come Saturday, and he can't wait to get in the car and disappear. Now, I'm the lawn care guy around here.

Wasn't always like this. Greg lived for the weekend, especially in the spring and summer. He'd do the lawn in the morning, maybe some errands with the kids in the early afternoon, later on get to a project in the woodworking shop he set up in the garage. Now here it is the middle of July and I haven't heard that band saw once this summer. And the only time I hear the lawn mower is when I turn it on 'cause Greg could care less about how the lawn was turning into a jungle of weeds. I used to love the weekends; we'd all be together, maybe doing our own things, but all here. Now he's always got something to do or check out, some reason not to be here. And, the truth is, even when he's here, he's not.

Rhonda N.

Most of us have broadly similar schedules, working five days a week and using the weekends to do the routine chores like grocery shopping, home maintenance, and hopefully enjoying some leisure activity like golf, visiting friends and family, or simply lounging around the house. But infidelity cuts a wide swath, even disrupting or altering the character of what your weekends have been.

Weekends can be particularly stressful for the cheater because he has little or no access to his lover. When the frustration of not being able to see or openly communicate with a lover reaches its peak, the cheater often will make excuses to be away from home, such as to look for a new gadget or pick up something at the office, all so he can call or even see his lover. As a consequence, the once normal routines are dispensed with by the cheater. This can extend to neglecting home and lawn maintenance, forfeiting minor repairs and keeping the lawn in shape. In fact, in just a matter of weeks, a home's appearance can deteriorate because the cheater's interest in attending to necessary chores has lagged because of his preoccupation with the affair. The untidy lawn and leaky faucets come to mirror the neglected, damaged marriage.

The Clues	The Meaning
• Leaves the house for hours on weekend	• Frustrated at not seeing his lover
• Neglects household, weekend chores	• His mind and priorities are somewhere else

New Interests in Which Little or No Enthusiasm Had Been Shown Before

I thought she didn't like foreign films. Now it's like she's a movie critic.

Because neither Emily nor I cared much for foreign films, if we'd see one on TV, we'd refer to those subtitles as "subtleties"—Emily thought that was a great joke because most of those kinds of films are just too philosophical or heady for us. She'd say people go to arty films just to act smart. And I kind of agree, not my kind of movie. But around the same time that she got her new job, Emily starts talking about this or that great foreign film we should rent from Blockbuster. How'd she even hear about these films? People at work, she says, talk about them all the time. So we rent some Japanese film, it's OK, then rent another, and I see Em's taking notes and even starts watching scenes over and over, talking about how the lighting does this and the arc of the plot is about that. Who's she kidding? And who's she trying to impress?

Raymond K.

Although most of us like to see ourselves open to learning about and experiencing new things, in actuality we remain pretty much set in our tastes and beliefs. That's not to say that you won't visit a Peruvian restaurant that recently opened or enjoy a song from a new rock group. But even if we don't rigidly hold to our ingrained personal tastes and preferences, they do pretty much stay with us throughout our adult lives. Our curiosity coupled with the availability of more leisure activities gives us the impetus to explore new things, engage in new hobbies, and pursue new interests. Though at the end of the day we'll likely still prefer, say, Italian food over other dining-out choices, romantic comedies over denser and more challenging films, and Carly Simon rather than a completely new genre of music. It's the same with the expressions and jargon we use— they pretty much remain the same over the years with new ones added only rarely. Changing our political views differs in that there are so many variables to factor in when deciding one's position on issues. Yet pollsters tell us that most people vote pretty much the same way their entire lives; they basically maintain their liberal or middle-of-the-road or conservative political leanings.

We're not saying that you or your spouse is inflexible and rigid. But what we are saying is that the tastes and preferences most of us develop over the years remain to a large degree consistent. Given this reality about most of us, you should carefully note any rather drastic and relatively sudden changes by your spouse in these areas. Though changes in the less-tangible areas, such as tastes and preferences, in the expressions he uses, or in his political outlook, might be subtler and more difficult to decipher, they are no less important and indicative of a possible affair than the appearance of those new and outlandishly loud shirts, or the new cologne and the bottle of Grecian Formula that suddenly appear on his bathroom shelf.

Often, a cheater becomes enamored not only with his lover but also with her tastes, outlook, expressions, and choice of movies and food. This affection for all things about her can then lead the cheater to emulate her, sometimes in the extreme. In one case, for example, our client was baffled when her husband, who was displaying a number of signs of cheating, became an ardent advocate of protecting bat habitats. That's right, bats. Here is a builder of shopping centers in southern New Jersey, someone who didn't even own a pet or particularly enjoy the outdoors, embracing the protection of flying mammals perched in New Mexican caves. Not that bat protection is not a worthy cause—we're sure it is. But in this case, it was another sign that he was closely involved with another person. When all was finally exposed, the client learned that her husband's lover was a member of a national bat habitat conservation organization.

Nuanced as most of these changes in tastes and beliefs are, careful observation can lead us to recognize them. To assist you in recognizing these changes, on p. 49 you'll find a chart of common changes in your partner's personal tastes and preferences over a wide variety of categories.

The Clues	The Meaning
• Sudden interest in new topics	• Inspired by his lover's interests
• Uses new expressions	• Emulating the way the lover speaks

Attitude—Change Signal Number Three: Uninvolved, Disinterested, and Distracted at Home

Often, obvious changes that suspecting wives notice in their husbands are *not* just what he's added to his life—new clothes hanging in the closet, extra working hours, sudden interest in topics he never cared about—but those things he's drastically reduced or eliminated from his life, such as the emotional involvement with his wife, family, and friends. Describing a change in her husband, one client said it was as if he had moved to a faraway country, never to be seen or heard from.

Although his body was still at home, his feelings, his concerns, his involvement with family and friends had been packed up and shipped to some distant place only he knew of. The following signs are typical of this kind of "distancing" signal that many of our clients see in their increasingly remote and uninvolved husband.

Hardly Any Sex, and Even Less Intimacy

The last time he touched me in bed was to nudge me to stop snoring.

But it wasn't always like that, not at all. Chris and I used to have what I always thought was a good sex life, I mean, we both enjoyed having sex; he never complained and neither did I for that matter. So sex was never an issue, was always a good part of our marriage. Now it's not anything, I mean nothing, zilch. Chris makes me feel like we're not supposed to have sex, like it's something that doesn't even belong in our relationship. Maybe four months ago, when it was becoming obvious that something had changed in our bedroom, I tried to talk about it and he blew up, also not like him at all, said it's natural, it happens in marriages and it'll pass, case closed. He's into bed earlier now, usually sleeping by the time I'm ready for bed, and he's up earlier too, says he likes working in the office before the other staff comes in. I still love him, and really pray this isn't what I think it is.

Lynne A.

As we pointed out earlier in this chapter, an increase in his sexual appetite at home can be a key Change Signal. But at the other extreme in sexual activity lies his almost total avoidance of sex. And in those rare cases when lovemaking occurs, the intimacy is totally absent. Of all the major warning signs, the diminishment of lovemaking and intimacy is among the most universal and blatant indicators of an affair.

While you might feel that this shifting of sexual affection from you is a consequence of his desire to have sex with the other person, it might not be as simple or as singular a reason as that. Also playing a possible role in this absence of sex from your relationship is the guilt the cheater feels, guilt that manifests itself in the cheater's denying sex with his legitimate partner. Whatever the reasons, the result is a void in your sex life together. Of course, if a vastly diminished sex life is the only sign you have, then other causes, such as impotency, have to be considered. But in most cases, if the husband shows no interest in sex or refuses to have sex or is markedly less affectionate during what little sex you do have, *and* you have gathered other warning signs that are separate from this one, then you need to regard the lack of sex and affection as a most serious indicator of cheating.

Virtually all couples experience inconsistencies in their sexual life together. But when one partner ceases to be interested in sex, either gradually or suddenly, this could signal that the disinterested spouse is having an affair. On its own, of course, a partner's waning sexual interest cannot and should not immediately and conclusively be taken as evidence that a lover has entered his life. There are myriad reasons why one partner exhibits a lack of sexual interest, from emotional issues to medical conditions to simple aging. Even work and family issues can contribute to a declining sex drive.

But when a dropoff of sexual interest—especially a precipitous decline—occurs in the midst of numerous other important clues of infidelity, then a suspecting spouse is right to assume that the end of a couple's sex life could likely be coinciding with her partner's affair.

The Clue	The Meaning
• The coldest of shoulders, especially in bed	• Your spouse is being gratified by the lover; guilt might also play a factor in your being shut out sexually

Becomes Quiet, and Turning Inward at Home

He hardly talks to me anymore. And when he does, I don't feel like he's speaking to me.

So strange, because Rich won my heart with the way he would speak about things that matter to him, really had a way of making himself understood. And he loves, or loved, talking about almost anything, politics, sports, any topic that interested him or not. I can't believe this is the same man I married twelve years ago. Now his vocabulary is mostly grunts, nods, or a wave of the hand, like he's lost the capacity of speech. Or he'll get by with the minimum he can say, like it's painful for him to have a conversation with me. It's a little different in public, but at home, he's zipped up most of the time. There's a tenseness surrounding him too, but how can I even ask him what's wrong? He'll just shrug his shoulders a little and walk away.

Alma C.

While a number of causes could lead a spouse to become increasingly taciturn and quiet at home—including depression, anxiety, and anger, either unrelated to or as a direct consequence of an affair—it is often the case that the maddening, tight-lipped man who refuses to engage in anything but the most basic and necessary conversation is having an affair. But more than just conversation with your spouse has vanished from your house: He might now also appear completely disinterested in topics that you or other family members would, in less troubled times, talk about at the dinner table. If you or someone in the family brings up one of those subjects, your spouse might either bark back some dismissive remark or merely shrug or answer in ways that suggest that conversation is pointless.

Appearing bored, tired, restless, distracted, and inattentive at home are frequently complementary signs of a spouse's tuning out the family. All bundled together, you should regard these Change Signals as strongly indicating not only his underlying unhappiness at home but the likelihood of his having an affair. The reason the spouse shows little interest in conversation or engagement of any sort can be because of numerous elements, almost all relating to the affair. He might be thwarting conversation because he's worried it might lead to his being questioned about this new, quiet, remote nature he's displaying. He might feel frustrated being at home surrounded by all the elements that are keeping him from being with his lover. Or his shame about the affair and anxiety about being caught could make him build a protective wall around himself, isolating him from those he knows he's deceiving. Or it could be all of the above and then some. But the net result, whatever the inspiration, is a change from what was likely a normal amount of talk at home to a home where talk (at least for one person) is all but absent.

The Clue	The Meaning
• Quiet, remote, has nothing to say	• Afraid you might bring up how he's changed, and/or he's feeling guilty and frustrated

Argues All the Time, and Almost Always Over Nothing

If I even look at him the wrong way, Buddy blows his stack.

And this from someone I used to call the "Gentle Giant." Buddy's six foot three, and I'd tell people that I fell for him on our second or third date when I saw him talk two guys at a bar out of getting into a fight—like I said, he's a gentle guy. Or was. Where's that Buddy now? When he comes home from work, which is getting later and later these days, it's no longer his "How's your day been, hon?" greeting with his little hug. At best, it's just silence or a grunt that I suppose means hello. At worst, though, it's a blowup, really like an explosion, usually over nothing, like almost every night now. Yesterday, it was Mattie leaving sections of his train set in the hall, the very same train set Buddy would plop down on the floor to play choo-choo with

Mattie just a couple of months ago. And though I never know what's going to set Buddy off, I think I know what is bugging him. And it's destroying us.

Ariane G.

One of the more obvious attitudinal changes is the arrival of those incessant and pointless (to you) arguments you suddenly seem to be having with your spouse. Arising almost out of thin air, the arguments are triggered by an event or circumstance that normally would not even have been worth discussing, let alone having a full-fledged, high-decibel-level argument over. Most of the arguments are one sided, started by the cheater, but both parties can make it escalate, as that's the nature of arguments. The cause can stem from his being stressed out over the affair, mingled with guilt. And the outbursts could be manifestations, loud ones, of his feeling trapped and unable to spend time with his lover. So while he keeps picking fights, that isn't the real battle you're facing here.

The Clues	The Meaning
• Getting into arguments easily	• Your spouse could be feeling anxious and guilty about the affair
• Arguments are becoming more and more constant	• Feeling trapped, your spouse's anger about not spending time with the lover is increasing
• The source of the argument is often trivial and vague	• The arguments are not about the topic, but about your spouse's frustrations

Runs Away from an Argument

I don't know what I said, but two seconds later, Jenny's storming out of the apartment.

And to tell you the truth, sometimes I'm glad to see her go—at least it'll be quiet here. It's like the same show every night now, I'm already home, mostly because Jenny's working late or says she's been out with her girlfriends, and maybe two minutes after she walks in we're already at it, and three minutes after that, she's out the door, yelling "I need a smoke!" or that she's going to her sister's. Then she's back in an hour, maybe two, and can even be in pretty good mood, but I'm sure not. I have my suspicions, and I'm thinking, one night, when she comes back after one of those scenes, she'll be walking into an empty apartment.

Christopher N.

You might feel your spouse is leaving home to escape from or defuse the tension during an argument. While in some instances those might be the reasons why he's bolting out the door and not returning for a few anguished hours, there's likely another more selfish and deceitful reason: It is a tactic to secure private time with the lover (either on the phone or in person). Make note of when these fights leading to short absences occur—if they appear to have some regularity, then there's good reason to suspect that your partner is orchestrating these battles in order to spend more time with the lover.

The Clues	The Meaning
• The argument escalates in an instant, followed by the spouse's leaving the premises	• The spouse really wants to leave to call or visit with the lover
• The spouse can be gone for an extended length of time, often one or two hours	• The spouse may claim this amount of time was needed to calm down but it is likely the time was spent talking on the phone with or visiting the lover
• The spouse returns, often in a relaxed, or even jovial mood	• The spouse has spent time speaking with or visiting the lover

No Time for You, for the Kids, or for Anyone Who Matters

My daughter asked me, "Is something wrong with Dad?" That really hurts.

It's especially painful because Alberto's been a terrific, doting father, and an affectionate, loving, I thought, husband. So this not talking to any of us, not asking Cassie how school was or not driving her to her riding lessons or not even looking at her when she's talking, it's just awful. I know it's bad between us now, he's even less involved with me than with Cassie or his parents or anyone. I thought maybe it's depression or something like that, but now I'm thinking it's something else. He's a bundle of nerves here, and I can see he can't get out of the house and off to work fast enough. I'll find the truth one way or another, because Cassie and I deserve better than this.

Jill M.

More than his conversation with family members can lessen in a home where a spouse has become a cheater. The time the spouse spends with the family, either with individual members or with the family as a whole, can also diminish. This distancing from the family can be particularly stressful on the children because they usually have no idea why they are being ignored by a parent. Children placed in such a situation, where seemingly overnight one of their parents has little interest in being around them or playing with them or answering their questions or displaying the myriad ways parents show love and concern, can suffer greatly but not necessarily openly. Sad as this consequence is for the children, the distancing goes beyond the front door, as a cheater who has changed from engaging normally with his family becomes someone who's chosen to be as silent as a Trappist monk with his own siblings, perhaps parents, extended family, and friends. In fact, it's not uncommon for us to hear a client say that she first noticed how great the change had become when relatives and close friends remarked that "Sam certainly seems quiet these days, everything OK?" If it comes to the point that even those not living under your roof notice that your (possibly cheating) spouse is acting extraordinarily quiet and distant these days, you *know* you're dealing not just with deep silence but with a major sign warning you of an affair.

The Clue	The Meaning
• Diminished interest in the kids	• His mind is elsewhere
• Ignores the kids' request to talk or play	• Kids remind him of his familial responsibilities

A Rose by Any Other Name

The third time he called me Laurie, that's her name, I almost blew it, but I kept my lid on, which was not easy.

Can't he even hear himself when he does that? The first time, I thought, oh well, Jordon talks to people at work all day, so it's not a big deal. A week later, out comes her name again, and he's oblivious. So I started adding in the other things, the lack of sex we've had over the last maybe two months, the late nights at the office, the call he got on his cell when we were at Home Depot a couple weekends ago and seemed so flustered. And now yesterday, he calls me Laurie again. It was all I could do not to say, "Hey, my name's Gillian, Gillian—that Laurie is the woman I think you're having an affair with!" But I counted to ten, breathed deeply and slowly, and I made it through. But three strikes, you know.

Gillian J.

Distraction is one of the primary Change Signals to consider. You might realize he is not reacting when you or a family member is talking to him or he is gazing at the TV, though obviously not noticing or caring about what he's watching. But a common consequence of this distracted state could take the form of calling you by the wrong name, likely *her* name. Countless clients of ours, women and men, reported that the spouse has called them by the name of the other person. Obviously caused by distraction, tension, and possibly a highly charged home environment, this miscall is so common we can almost assure a client that there's a high likelihood it will happen or already has happened to them. If your spouse does call you by another name, try your best not to overreact (we know, this will be hard), especially if you haven't yet confronted your spouse with the accusation that he's having an affair. Being called by another name without questioning him about it—"*What* name did you just call me?"—will have great benefits, as it can help confirm that yes he's having an affair, and *this* is the name of the other person. Of course, people with good intentions make speaking mistakes all the time, including calling someone, including one's spouse, by the wrong name. Even Secretary of State Condoleezza Rice referred to her boss, President George W. Bush, as "my husband." If she can make a misstatement like that, anyone can. But when you're already harboring suspicions about your spouse, and he calls you by another woman's name, it's far more than an incorrect although embarrassing misstatement (as Rice's was)—it's a sign that your spouse could be having an affair.

The Clue	The Meaning
• Calls you by the lover's name	• Thinking of her
	• Stressed out because of the affair

Loss of Interest in Watching or Participating in Sports
He used to be a sports nut, but now he couldn't care less.

And I'm talking all-around sports fanatic here, baseball in the summer, football in the fall, basketball in the spring, and even though we live on the west coast of Florida, Jesse was crazy about hockey too. His favorite TV channel, seems like his only channel, was ESPN. And he didn't just watch sports—he played golf at least twice a week except in August. But the game's over. If he's home in time for Monday Night Football, *which is rare, as he's "working late," he's too tired to watch. And since he says he's got so many "chores" on weekends, his golf clubs are sitting in the front closet. Jesse's got himself another passion, I'm sure, so now I have to take the right actions to give this marriage a sporting chance.*

Ellie S.

When an affair takes hold of a person's life, other interests and passions can take a back seat. Or in many cases, they can be disposed of entirely. We've heard of season ticket holders skipping games, die-hard weekend tennis players whose racquets hang idly on the garage wall, and avid hunters who never remove their hunting arms from the case. You could assume that in instances like these, the people are trading their sports passion for another passion—the affair.

Most affairs require a large amount of effort and time. Something has to give, and the trade-off occurs because the cheater usually can't keep every element in life intact and at the same time maintain a full-fledged affair. Not that sports activities, including being a sports fan, are so readily expendable from a person's life. But we often see cheaters either significantly reducing or entirely eliminating sports to allow more time to conduct the affair.

The lack of involvement with once popular sports activities can also be the direct effect of the anxiety, depression, and stress that plague the cheater. In short, he's in no mood to enjoy watching or participating in sports. But whatever the reason for the game being over as far as sports, you'd be smart to see it as a sign that other games are being played.

The Clue	The Meaning
• No longer an avid sports fan	• Anxious, depressed, stressed out
• Affair takes up his free time	• Doesn't play or engage in sports or outdoor activities

No Longer Interested in Doing Things with You

We used to do everything together. Now our duet is made up of two solo acts.

Even when Amanda and I are together, like when we're grocery shopping, we're not really together, not like we used to be. People used to joke how we'd finish each other's sentences. And I'd always know where she'd want to go out to dinner, and Amanda would never fail to get me the right gift. No more two peas in a pod, not anywhere close to it. We used to walk the dog to the lake together right after dinner, but now I take Bruiser out by myself. I can tell Amanda doesn't even want me in the same room with her—she leaves the den if I happen to sit down to read near her. No fights, no nasty talk, but a real separation within the house and out of the house has sneaked into our lives together, or I mean not together. I know Amanda's mind is somewhere else, thinking of someone else, and I'm left feeling even lonelier.

Jonathan L.

Shopping, going to movies, planting the vegetable garden, walking the dog, redecorating your kids' rooms, and the thousand of other activities people who live together engage in make a couple really a couple. And you begin to sense, one by one, that these activities you once did jointly are now done separately or they're not done at all. Perhaps the two of you still catch a movie together, but even at those times it doesn't feel as a "we" or "us," but more as a "me" and "him." You might have noticed this as a creeping parting, or perhaps it happened more quickly in a matter of weeks. But no matter what the duration, the cause can likely be because your spouse is seeing someone else he wants to be with for now. The more things the two of you do together, the more confined your spouse might feel. So he chooses to do on his own those things the two of you had always performed together, as a couple, a team. He might deny that this obvious migration from your joint activities to this solo performance is even happening. But the more often you find yourself alone in an activity where he was usually at your side, the more reason you have to be suspicious.

The Clue	The Meaning
• You're alone in things you used to do together	• His mind is on the affair • He doesn't want to feel attached

Turning to Dr. Gunzburg: The Six Emotions You Will Face

The Change Signals that Tony and Dawn and their clients describe here, individually and in combination with others, can help reveal if your partner is cheating. But if and when the Change Signals prove to be accurate and you're almost positive you are living with a cheater, how do you handle that? How do you deal with the reality that all the Change Signals, as well as your suspicions and fears, were all true and not a construction of your overactive imagination? Recognizing and dealing with your own emotions—and here I identify and discuss the six most important ones—is the first step in learning how to effectively and constructively deal with the revelations and the aftermath of an affair.

Betrayal

Betrayal is the most obvious emotion, the leader of the pack, the one that all the others we'll be discussing follow, the one that's at the heart and core of adultery. What is it that makes betrayal such an all-powerful emotion? When you are in an intimate relationship, when you are willing and expected to expose, literally, everything about yourself to the other person, the only way to successfully, willingly and lovingly do that is by giving the other person your total trust; when that trust is assaulted in the worst way possible—your partner is having an affair—it is not just your trust that has been violated. The most intimate and personal parts of you have been violated, so you might question your attractiveness, your personality, your humor—anything or everything about yourself.

To deal with this powerful emotion, it's helpful to write down your thoughts—literally put pen to paper or type it on your computer—so you can review and reflect upon them. Yes you were cheated on; that's not news, but ask yourself on paper what is most hurtful and hard to live with about your spouse's infidelity. How are you expressing your hurt feelings to yourself? And how are you expressing that hurt to others?

Guilt

The second emotion, guilt, is not your partner's feelings of guilt but *your* guilt. If you are like many of my patients, you feel the affair happened because of something or many things you did or didn't do. But the fact is, you aren't the one who had the affair, you didn't break the sacred trust, you didn't cause this enormous pain to you partner. Even if your words and behavior contributed to making a "bad" marriage, you did not cross the betrayal line. The affair is one person's decision and behavior and it should never have happened regardless of how bad your marriage was or how bad your behavior was (if that is the case). Many of my patients say they would have described their marriage as good, and sometimes wonderful, prior to knowing about the affair. For yourself, you have to figure out why you still feel guilty.

First consider where guilt comes from. It's actually a normal and expected response formed in our unconscious. Our unconscious mind works in what might seem like mysterious ways, but it's working for us. In the case of guilt, the role of our unconscious is to force us to weigh our current, previous, or future actions against what we regard as right or wrong. And you likely do feel guilty about the affair. Why? I can't tell you, but you can. In thinking about your marriage, pay attention to those things you have done right and those things you consider that you have done wrong. There's a good chance you'll be able to get a sense of what it is that's making you feel guilty. Sure, you weren't the perfect spouse, no one is. But nothing you did caused him to cheat on you. It's not your fault, regardless of how much your spouse might say it's your fault, and regardless of how much you might feel it is.

To deal with these feelings of guilt, write down what drives the feeling in you. Then for every reason, write down your argument against it. Remember that you were not consulted about having the affair—it was a one-sided decision. The more you do this, the more you'll recognize that you are not the guilty one.

Disappointment

You'll also deal with major disappointment. Of course you should feel disappointed—after all, you've been cheated on, and the results of everything you've worked so hard to achieve are in shambles. Even if you are now questioning whether you worked hard at your marriage, whatever you thought at the time is no longer true and leaves you with disappointment instead of an active marriage. You might also feel a large sense of self-disappointment. You could even carry this over to feeling disappointed in the whole human race—you look around and everything and everybody has become one big disappointment.

These feelings are perfectly normal. You have been traumatized. Something has happened (your partner's infidelity) that is so completely outside your realm of possibility that you are devastated. The danger is in allowing your disappointment to spiral out of control, leaving you feeling despondent and totally hopeless. Watch yourself here. Disappointment is a normal emotion. Feeling completely and utterly hopeless is allowing your disappointment to gain a powerful and debilitating hold over you. To help you handle the emotion of disappointment, write down all that you're feeling disappointed about. You might feel you will never recover, but for almost everyone, time helps to heal disappointment. Go through your list and after each disappointment, write what holding on to that disappointment will do for you, and what letting go of it will do for you.

For example, if you wrote for one of your items, "I am so disappointed that our last anniversary was just a sham—I thought we had such a wonderful bonding experience."

When you write what holding on to that disappointment does for you, you might say, "When I think of this deception happening at such a special time, our anniversary, it keeps me from trusting any special times we might have. I think I need that thought as protection right now."

And for what will letting go of this do for you? "If I would let go of this disappointment, I would be making myself vulnerable again, but I would also be making future bonding experiences possible again. I don't feel ready to be that vulnerable."

Anger

Anger, another common emotion, overlaps a sense of betrayal. No wonder, because these two emotions are closely linked—betrayal leads most people to anger. When your spouse had an affair, he acted like a true enemy against you. The primitive response to encountering a true enemy is anger and rage. Don't let the depths of your anger and rage frighten you or make you feel you're out of control. Feeling angry and doing something while angry are different. You are responsible for your own behavior: Don't do anything that could harm yourself or others, and don't do anything you will later regret.

Even if anger leads to disturbing ideas, thoughts you never imagined yourself capable of conceiving, these are just thoughts, and they are a manifestation of the trauma you are recovering from. It is understandable if you have thoughts of your spouse and lover's suffering so they will understand the pain and hurt that has been afflicted on you. You might like them to hurt as much as you do. These are fantasies. Refrain from anything that could cause pain to others, because if you create another's pain, it will likely come back to haunt and possibly hurt you. It simply is not worth it. Think bad thoughts, but do not act on them.

If you feel like you might want to do what's in your mind, then immediately put this book down and seek the help of a psychologist or psychiatrist. You might need some medication to help you through these early days after the discovery of the infidelity. This is not a joking matter. Please follow through on this if you think you are at risk of acting on your vengeful thoughts. Writing your thoughts and feelings in a notebook can be an effective way of managing your feelings. If you still feel overwhelmed by your feelings, it helps to talk them out—with a close friend or relative, or with a psychologist.

Fear

Fear, too, is part of the process of dealing with the aftermath of a cheating partner. Fear can cover the spectrum, from fear that everything you thought you had is now gone forever to fear that the relationship can't be salvaged to fear that this isn't the last time this is going to happen.

You might even have some fears that everybody and everything is working against you. As extreme as this fear is, it is logical; after all, your world's been turned upside down. Maintain a "Fear" section in your notebook and write down your thoughts and feelings concerning your fears. Go back and determine which fears are way out and which ones could realistically happen. Write out what you're thinking in a thoughtful manner, and then think about what might help you alleviate each fear. Write down these potential solutions. Don't limit yourself to one analysis or one potential solution for each fear but stretch your mind for alternatives. You should know that for all writing exercises you should not expect to do each one once and move on. Rather, these are done over time, revisiting what you have already written and adding to it as you arrive at more information.

Paranoia

And finally, you could very likely feel paranoid. But let me first emphasize that I am using the layperson's definition of the word paranoid, meaning bothersome suspicious feelings, and not a chronic state of paranoia. You have been very hurt, so it's only natural to feel paranoid or suspicious, especially of the person who severely hurt you. If the affair has been exposed—or when it is finally exposed—you will need assurances from the cheater that it's over and it won't happen again. In my experience, that will not be enough to calm your suspicions. Also, you might find your paranoid feelings spilling over to other relationships and, more generally, to your worldview. These experiences are within the normal range for someone who was traumatized by an affair.

Change Signals: What to Look For

The four most important characteristics that all Change Signals share are (1) the changes cover a gamut of alterations, from how the husband looks to his embracing new activities to displaying a markedly different attitude and temperament; (2) these changes are inspired by and are a direct consequence of the husband's having an affair—they certainly didn't occur spontaneously and for no reason, even if it at first it seems that way; (3) each change is an overtly personal one for the individual, one that affects how he looks or is perceived by others; and (4) with most Change Signals, their occurrence overlaps each other, making them seem to appear pretty much altogether.

Because the dozens of Change Signals cover such a wide range of areas, you might feel you won't be able to track every one of them. That's why we give our clients the following Change Signals Map and Reference Guide (p. 49).

1. Change Signals in Appearance

a. He's become consumed with wearing clothes which, to him at least, make him look younger and perhaps sexier or more masculine; if possible, see if he wears the new clothes on those days you suspect, from other Warning signs, that he's having an affair.

b. Getting rid of his gray hair with hair color, especially if he's never discussed it with you or tried it before, can be an important Change Signal—the same goes for his growing a moustache or beard, or shaving them off after having had them for years, all without mentioning it to you beforehand.

c. As new creams, bronzers, tanning bottles and, frequently, a new cologne, suddenly show up, this marked increase in grooming time and attention is a signal worth noting.

2. Change Signals in Activities

a. He's become concerned, even obsessed, with getting in shape, starting with joining a gym—and you've never before seen the passion and dedication he's displaying for turning buff.

b. Losing weight has become a serious concern to him, one that you've never seen him pursue with such dedication—this sign gains in importance when coupled with other Change Signals and Warning signs.

c. An increase in lovemaking may be accompanied with new sexual positions and the introduction of sex toys; ironically, the added sex is more than offset by a lack of affection during lovemaking.

d. Losing interest in or simply neglecting home chores, especially those often attended to on the weekend (when he has less contact with his lover), is a common Change Signal, though one that takes longer to notice.

e. He shows strong, even passionate interest in topics or items that seem to both appear out of the blue and are not the kinds of things you'd think he would care about —they're likely inspired by his lover.

3. Change Signals in Attitude

a. The lack of sex, either its being greatly diminished or completely eliminated, is one of the most telling of all the Change Signals; there may be other causes, but when the avoidance of sex is accompanied by other Change Signals and Warning signs, odds are an affair's going on.

b. When you can count the number of words he says in an evening on one hand, he's likely got other things, such as an affair, on his mind; his unwillingness to talk can extend to every member of the family, and to friends and associates.

c. He might inadvertently change how he addresses you, calling you by his lover's name, because his lover is often on his mind when he's not with her.

THE MAJOR CHANGE SIGNALS

HIS APPEARANCE

- Buying new clothes
  Expensive
  Fashionable
  Youthful/Hip
  Tailored suits

- New hairstyle
  Youthful cut
  New color
  Covers gray

- Grooming more

- Grows/shaves
  Moustache
  Beard

- New eyeglasses
  Contacts
  Lasik

- Teeth whitened

- Tanning salon

- Skin products
  Bronzer
  Moisturizers

- New cologne

HIS ACTIVITIES

- Getting in shape
  Joining a gym
  Jogging
  Working out

- Dieting
  Serious plan
  More dedicated

- More sex
  But less intimate
  New techniques

- Weekend routine
  alters

- Less concern for
  home maintenance

- New expressions

- New tastes in:
  Movies
  Books
  TV shows

- Different politics
  Change in ideas
  New causes

- Leaves earlier for
  work

HIS ATTITUDE

- Less sex
  Or no sex

- Talks less
  Disinterested
  Appears bored
  Laughs less
  Distracted

- Less family time

- Becomes remote
  from family

- Distancing from
  friends

- Calls you by
  another name

- Loss of interest in
  sports/sports
  teams

- Not as attentive to
  the kids

- Diminished interest
  in joint activities

Many if not most of the major Change Signals are displayed right in your home. But there are other kinds of signals—body signals—that can also betray your spouse's guilt.

CHAPTER 3
The Body of Truth

Here's the good news about being lied to by your husband: He's probably not very good at it. Call him what you will right now, but chances are you're not married to a pathological liar—a person who suffers from a mental disorder that manifests itself by the compulsive need to lie and whose lies are so well delivered, most of us could not detect them. But the majority of people are simply lousy liars. Their deceitfulness can be made apparent to you—if you know what to look for, listen to, and pay special attention to—because their body language will often tell you when they're lying.

We're not saying that it will be easy for you to become a human lie detector. It will demand that you learn the key indicators exhibited by someone who is telling a lie and that you don't let on that you suspect your smiling husband is lying through his teeth. And it will take patience on your part to accumulate the evidence of his lying: You may need to have a number of conversations with your husband to give him the opportunity to tell a large enough body of substantial lies to prove that he's having an affair. But we can assure you that with the lie-detection signs we're about to share with you, you'll be able to determine—though no one can say with 100 percent assurance—if what he's telling you is the truth or one more lie.

We've seen many technological advances in our pursuit of the truth for clients over the years—from tiny video cameras that fit in a pen to portable listening devices that can pick up a conversation one hundred yards away to computer spyware and global positioning systems (GPS) that pinpoint a person's location to within a few feet. But in our decades in this field, one highly effective area of investigation hasn't been improved upon, an area that ironically is not based on technology or requires any technical expertise whatsoever. But when used properly, this investigative device can provide evidence of an affair as thoroughly, accurately, and consistently as the fanciest digital equipment ever could. The device is *you*—and your ability to read a person's body language for signs of lying. We call this area of investigation the Body of Truth, because his body language, more than virtually anything else he's saying, is your window into knowing whether what he's saying is the honest truth or a flat-out lie.

How to Listen to What His Body Is Telling You

If you suspect your partner of cheating, it's only natural that you'll be suspicious of what he tells you, especially in those areas and topics that hold the most interest to you, such as his late working hours. Where exactly *was* he last Saturday afternoon? And why did he call you by another woman's name? But be careful. If you believe that there's nothing you *can* believe, then it will be much harder for you to separate the truth from his deceitful answers. It's far better to trust what his body language is telling you than to feel that everything he says to you is dishonest. You're searching for the truth, wherever that might lead you, so give it a chance. This approach will allow you to far more accurately distinguish between fact and fiction.

Like any language, body language is full of nuance and idioms and has many parts. But from what we've learned working with experts we've consulted with over the years on the topic of body language and lying, reading body language falls into two main areas: the actual movement of the individual's body parts (the eyes, mouth, hands, feet, legs, and of course the whole body) and how the person speaks, including his or her tone of voice and speech patterns.

A Body of Lies

Of the two areas—the body and speech—the body generally reveals more, mainly because it provides more signals to look for and more ways for a liar to unwittingly betray the fact that he's not telling the truth.

Let's start at the top. The face of a person telling a lie often appears less animated than that of someone telling the truth. What movement there is, is limited to the mouth, not the eyes, which normally move in concert with the mouth—for example, when you smile, your eyes smile too, getting wider as your lips form a smile. A person who's lying is usually tight lipped, with the corners of the mouth turned down. Darting eyes can also serve as a reliable sign of someone's lying, so much so that many liars make a concerted effort *not* to move their eyes or blink excessively. So a blank, fixed stare—the opposite of darting, blinking eyes—can indicate a dishonest response as well.

The face has other ways of revealing dishonesty to you. Blushing and sweating remain classic signs of lying, both physical reactions to the emotional strain that lying places on the psyche. But at the other end of the facial spectrum is a face that is actually drained of color, as some liars become so anxious about their deceitfulness that it constrains the blood flow to their skin. So, oddly, bright red and pale white are both signs of lying.

Monkeying Around with the Truth

There they sit, the three wise monkeys, one with its hands over its ears, another with hands hiding its eyes, and the third monkey covering its mouth. And of course you know the expression that goes with this iconic Japanese image: Hear no evil, see no evil, speak no evil. Perhaps these three wise monkeys have become universally known because they exhibit precisely the signs we humans make when we're *not* telling the truth. Psychologists and students of body language (including groups as diverse as human resources professionals and law enforcement investigators) look for these "hand-to-head" movements as indicators of lying.

For example, a liar will often put his hand near his mouth, as if to cover up the mouth and the lie. He may also touch the face near his eyes or even begin rubbing his eyes when speaking an untruth. The ears too come into play, with liars frequently tugging at an ear lobe or actually scratching the inside of the ear. Finally, even the nose can display subtle telltale signs of lying (remember Pinocchio?), with liars often pulling it or rubbing it as if they're about to sneeze. Some liars wrinkle their noses ever so slightly and usually very quickly when telling a lie, giving the impression that something smells bad (like what they're saying, for instance). Flaring the nostrils can also be a sign that you shouldn't believe what you hear. Each of these hand-to-head gestures and actions can be a result of the stress and anxiety one feels because of telling a lie.

Eyes and Lies

Darting eyes, as we've said, are a strong sign of lying behavior, as are firmly fixed eyes. But there are two eye movements you may not associate with lying. First, and this may sound odd, but please do what we ask—we want you to recall the name of the last movie you saw. Chances are in thinking about the answer, your eyes moved up and to the left. That's where most of us move our eyes when we're trying to recall a fact, when we're thinking of something from the past. Eyes up and to the left. Now, we want you to think about what you're planning on doing this upcoming weekend. OK, where did your eyes move?

Up, yes, but this time to your right. That's the eye movement most of us make when we're thinking about the future. Up and to the right.

Here's how you can use that knowledge of universal eye movements to help you determine if you're being lied to: At the appropriate moment, ask the suspected cheater a question relating to an event you're particularly suspicious of. For example, if he told you he was working late last night and you suspect he was really with his lover, ask him a question that would require a specific answer that includes some detail, such as, "So, what exactly were you working on last night?" If he indeed did work on the new marketing plan, his eyes will go up and to his left, the position of recall. But if his eyes go up to his right, he's thinking of something that hasn't happened, and he's forming an answer, not recalling an actual event. In other words, he's lying. While not a foolproof test of honesty (as you might not ask a question that lends itself to a specific answer), it is an uncannily reliable tool. If you do employ this tactic a few times, and in every instance, instead of his eyes moving to the recall position of up and to his left they move to the "future" position of up and to the right, you can feel confident that he's lying.

Body Signals

Other body signs to watch for include agitated movement of the hands, arms, feet, and legs. Because a liar feels tense and nervous, his hands and feet tend to move with more frequency and often in rather jerky, awkward ways. Along with these motions, notice if he rhythmically opens and closes his hands or places them in his pockets (to hide how nervous he feels). Placing his palms downward may also indicate that he's not telling the truth. (The opposite movement, placing your opened palms so they face the other person, is an almost universal sign of innocence saying, "You can believe me.")

Even if your spouse manages to still his hand movements, you may instead notice that he's doing the liar's shuffle, tapping his feet nervously, or that he's crossing and uncrossing his legs at a fast rate. Both are signs of anxiety brought on by having to conceal the truth. Also watch for the full body movement—usually away from you. If you happen to be sitting next to him while he's lying, he may shoot up and move across the room, because it's harder to lie to someone who's in close proximity—the farther away, the easier it is to lie.

Few of us relish telling a lie. This is why a person who is lying will often turn his head, and sometimes his entire body, away from the person the lie is directed to. To feel additional protection while telling a lie, it's also common for the liar to place symbolic barriers between himself and the person being fed the untruths, including folding his arms over his chest in a defensive motion or crossing his legs tightly. The barriers don't have to be part of his body either; he might place a newspaper, coffee cup, eyeglasses, or some other object directly between himself and the victim of his lies.

And there's a polar opposite to all of this toe-tapping, arm-folding, and leg-crossing activity: A stiff stance or equally rigid sitting position is a sign of intense discomfort with the situation, and himself, because of his lying. The rigidity can also be a function of his not wanting to display any suspicious signs at all. In fact, he performs the wooden soldier look to make himself appear sober and honest. But you'll know better.

How to Sound Out a Lie

While you're looking at how he moves his hands, eyes, and even his nostrils, keep your own ears open. It's not simply the words he's uttering that matter, but just as important— in fact, probably *more* important—is the manner in which he's delivering those words. His words are just that, words; but his *manner* of speaking when lying is what can tell you if the words are true or not.

For example, if his response to questions takes longer to form than usual, he's probably using the extra time to fabricate a lie. A truthful response is almost automatically delivered without pause; a lie follows a noticeable pause, because he forms the lie rather than immediately stating the simple truth. Besides taking longer to answer when the answer is a lie, it will often be delivered in a higher-pitched voice. And this is true even if the liar is six foot three and a deep baritone. The very act of lying makes us nervous, and the tension can affect the vocal chords, stretching them more than usual, resulting in a higher-pitched voice.

Going from a baritone to a tenor isn't the only difference in his delivery. Liars often garble their answers and not as a ploy to disorient or confound you. Lies confuse the liar's own brain, so the first letters of consecutive words or entire words might be switched. Other speech errors occur, from leaving out words to mispronouncing simple words. The liar sounds flustered and nervous because that's precisely what he is.

Also, because lying is such a difficult act for us to perform with any semblance of adroitness, the answers liars give are frequently in the form of abbreviated expressions, not the usual kind of fluid sentences we expect. Even if your partner happens to be the taciturn type, a man of few words, you should be able to discern a difference between his usual way of speaking and the short, one- or two-word responses that he's now prone to give.

The Echo Effect

Most liars share the interesting trait of answering a question using the identical words of the question. So if you ask him, "Were you at the bar again with those friends of yours?" he might respond, "No, I was not at the bar again with those friends of mine." It's simply easier for a liar to repeat a question verbatim rather than forming an honest response.

Another clue that you're hearing a lie is the use of full words rather than the more conversational contraction. For example, rather than say "I wasn't out to lunch for two and a half hours," he'll say, "I was not out to lunch for two and a half hours." By forgoing the contraction he's attempting to make the lie sound more truthful. Along the same line, liars attempt to enhance the believability of their lies by layering them with an overabundance of information, supplying far more details than are needed or that they normally use. Moreover, many liars speak in a monotone when lying in an effort to appear unemotional or calm. One way to confirm in your own mind that his tone is indeed flatter than usual (and therefore evidence of his lying) is to notice if the pronouns he uses—I, you, she, me, and so on—have more emphasis or not over the rest of the words in a sentence. Generally, pronouns are given more emphasis when we speak, so if they sound as flat as the rest of the sentence, *he* might be telling *you* flat-out lies about *her.*

A Quick Lie Detector

To increase your arsenal of ways to sense if he's lying or telling the truth, use this quick test: Let's say during one of your more intense conversations in which you're dead certain he's giving you one lie after another, suddenly change to a completely benign, innocuous topic, and notice where he goes with it. If he's been lying during this conversation, he'll immediately feel less stressed, more relieved, and eager to pursue this far less-intimidating, troubling topic. But if he wasn't lying, he'll likely not want to change topics so readily. Just be prepared: Odds are, he's going to be very happy to switch to topics that seem to get him off the hook (which will only prove just how much of a liar he really is).

Numbers Don't Lie, Liars Lie

Not all of his lies can be detected from his body language or the tone and tenor of his voice. Other lies are communicated by such inanimate objects as his car's odometer, which can tell you that he's been lying about what you suspect has been going on.

For example, his car's odometer can inform you that on those days that he claims he's working late, he's actually spending time in the car driving to, well, somewhere that he doesn't want you to know about. Chances are your husband's daily work-week driving pattern is pretty consistent. (If he's a salesman on the road or commutes by rail, then focus on his weekend driving patterns.) This means the total number of miles he drives during the week remains pretty much the same. But if he says he's working late on Tuesday, and the odometer has an extra ten or fifteen miles on it, you're right to be suspicious. Or let's say on Saturday afternoon he says he's going to run a couple of errands, but in completing those chores he adds an extra thirty miles of driving, then consider the possibility that he's likely done more than stop by the local Home Depot.

Calculating these additional miles requires some elemental sleuthing on your part to check his odometer reading. Of course, you'll have to do this when he's not aware of it. First, you need a benchmark mileage reading, so on a day when you're confident that his mileage represents a normal day's driving, check the odometer in the morning (or the night before) and again after he comes home. Do this a couple of times to accurately estimate the average mileage driven on a typical workday or weekend day. That's your benchmark reading. Then on a work night when he's "working late," check the mileage, perhaps early the next morning when he's in the shower or is otherwise unaware that you're in the car jotting down the odometer reading, to compare it to the normal bench-mark. If he is indeed working all those extra hours, you should see no significant change in the mileage—after all, the car was parked at his workplace. But if more miles consistently appear to accumulate on those days he says he's working late (or early), then the odometer is displaying not just numbers, but a serious warning sign.

Taking Off the Ring

Another sign of lying about keeping his marriage vows is the very symbol of the marriage itself, his wedding band. If your spouse suddenly *loses* his ring or *forgets* to wear it, it can be a blatant message that he's either trying to conceal his mar-riage from someone or that he wants to avoid rubbing it in his lover's face. Taking off his wedding band may also give him a temporary sense of freedom, enabling him to escape from the physical reminder of his marriage when he's not at home.

A client of ours, Sandra P., told us that her husband's wed-ding band made her become suspicious that he might be hav-ing an affair or at least was thinking about it. Here's her story, as she related it to us:

Out of the complete blue, and after twenty-two years of marriage, Ron just stops wearing his wedding ring. "It's too tight," he tells me when I notice the ring's not on his finger. So I think this is no big deal and tell him we'll go to a jeweler I like a lot and have the ring enlarged. Ron says he's got no time for jewelers. OK, OK, I say, 'cause I can see he's got better things to do. So a few days later, I'm thinking that our anni-versary's coming up in a week, so as a surprise to Ron I'll get his ring enlarged. I take the ring from his jewelry case where he had plopped it near his college ring and some cuff links, both of which I haven't seen him wear in years, and stop by the jeweler's to have it enlarged one size up. Ron doesn't notice of course that it's not in his jewelry case, and come our anniversary, we go out to dinner like always. Dessert comes and I take out this little gift-wrapped box, tell him happy anniversary, he opens it and asks, with no smile, "What's this, my ring?" I say yes and now it should fit. He just twirls the ring around in his fingers, doesn't put it on, so I say, "Honey, put it on, it should fit perfectly." After some hemming and hawing he slips it on, and it's a size too big, way too loose! I knew, whoa, something doesn't make sense here, but I say let's have it resized again, but Ron kind of dismisses the whole thing, says not to bother, 'cause the ring also had been irritating his skin. By then I knew that Ron didn't want to let the world, or someone, know that he was a married man.

After this, Sandra employed a number of the same tools you've seen in *Warning Signs* that confirmed that he had been having an affair. Our investigator found out that the other woman had thought Ron was a widower—and widowers, as we know, don't wear wedding rings.

There's a good chance that untruths aren't coming only from your husband, for as Dr. Gunzburg reveals, some distortions of the facts actually originate from your own negative thoughts and erroneous self-talk. How to recognize and challenge your mind's distortions of reality will help you overcome and remove them from your life.

Turning to Dr. Gunzburg: How to Deal with Your Own Negative Thinking

Everyone dislikes being lied to, especially when the lies and distortions come from the person you thought was your most trusted friend, your spouse. Almost all cheaters, though, try to cover up or deny an affair. If you are like most couples, there will be plenty of lies and distortions from your spouse. Believe it or not, your attitude could make it seem worse. Your negative filter might create a lie out of an honestly mistaken memory, or your fantasies might be so strong you confuse them with what really happened.

Should you find yourself trying to cope with what might seem like an onslaught of negative thinking, the following can be highly effective in disproving this negative thinking while substituting the negativity and distortions with positive thoughts of your self-image and self-worth.

The first step is to track down negative thoughts that are causing you to feel bad—and incorrectly—about yourself. You probably understand that thinking negatively can actually affect how you feel. Thinking precedes feeling, although it can happen so fast you might not notice the thinking. Also, after you find out about an affair, you have set up a prejudgment or attitude so you have prethought most situations. You're ready to have a bad feeling based on your prethought-out attitude.

If you are tired of contributing your own negative thoughts to the awfulness of your situation, then I recommend you think of and write down at least three or four scenes in which you feel really good about yourself—preferably without your spouse. These scenes could be from your work world, from your childhood, your family or friends, or from a time when you were alone. They might involve an achievement, a kindness or thoughtful act, a creative solution you offered, a physical achievement, or just a time when you felt really good about yourself. Carry the list with you. Anytime you have one of the bothersome thoughts, pinch yourself or snap yourself with a rubber band or step on your own toe (do not cause pain, just discomfort), and then in the moment when the bothersome thought goes away, mentally put yourself into one of the situations where you feel really good about yourself.

Here's an example. Say you're jogging along the running path in the park as you do every weekend, and you spot a man and a woman on a park bench. You immediately think, "That must be how my husband and his lover meet," and the idea of it makes you think how your husband can't wait to get out of the house to meet his lover secretly like this. You think, "I'm so unappealing, he's just itching to get away from me to meet her." Reach over and pinch yourself. In that moment when your mind is distracted from what you were thinking, imagine the time when you helped a disabled person make a trip to the grocery store, and step into the good feeling you had about yourself. Of course you can always argue with yourself about any bothersome thought by asking the following questions:

- Just how much sense does this thought really make, and how believable is it in the real world?
- Can I make a logical, realistic argument against this thought?
- How much real, true, accurate evidence and facts exist that prove the thought is true?
- And, let's say the thought is in fact true, how would that meaningfully affect my life at this moment?

In creating your arguments against your own problem thinking, learn to recognize thoughts that are almost always a problem, such as,

- Thoughts that are categorical, using words like "always," or "absolutely," or "never"—such as, "I'll always be the loser" or "He'll never change."
- Thoughts that put labels on things, such as "What an idiot I am" or "He's a bum." In truth, Forrest Gump had it right—"Stupid is as stupid does," meaning that an act can be stupid, but that doesn't make the person stupid.
- Thoughts that exist in the extreme, such as "I'm the most awful listener on Earth" or "He's worse than any man I've ever known."

- Thoughts on reprisals, such as a person who did something wrong having to suffer the consequences no matter what.
- Thoughts on your controlling it all, meaning the situation must go only how you want it to, or else.
- Thoughts on outside pressures that are out of your control but are nonetheless controlling your life and your problems.
- Thoughts that give poor excuses or weak reasons why things are the way they are.
- Thoughts built around utter hopelessness—"It's terrible now, it was always bad, and things aren't going to be getting any better in the future."
- Thoughts demanding that a resolution and answers be found or you will suffer.

It's likely that at least a few of these kinds of negative thoughts will appear in your mind but in their own way of course. If they do, immediately try to recognize them for what they are—negative and potentially harmful thoughts—and then challenge them to the reality test. Their strength and power will fade dramatically, and you'll be the stronger for causing that to happen.

While you're working on your bothersome thoughts, you might fill in with more positive thoughts. Make a list of positive and energizing statements that refer to your strengths. Put each on an index card and carry the stack with you. During any lull in your day, go through a few cards saying out loud the statement on each card and think positively. These are called "affirmations" and have been used successfully for generations. An example would be, "I've done difficult things before, and I am going to get through this time successfully," or "I am a loving and loveable person who . . ."

THE WARNING SIGNS
LIE DETECTION GUIDE

Watch his . . .	For signs of:	Checklist

Eyes
- Darting —————
- Avoiding your eyes —————
- Staring intently into your eyes —————
- Pupils getting larger —————
- Frequently blinking —————
- Moves eyes up and to his right when "recalling" facts —————

Nose
- Wrinkles nose when speaking —————
- Rubs nose —————

Mouth
- Hands in front of mouth —————
- Lips tightened —————

Overall Face
- Blank expession —————
- Frozen —————
- Flushed —————
- Sweating —————

THE WARNING SIGNS
LIE DETECTION GUIDE

Watch his . . .	For signs of:	Checklist
Hands and fingers	• Moves hands frequently and awkwardly	_____
	• Places hands in front of mouth	_____
	• Crosses hands in front of himself	_____
	• Open and closes hands frequently	_____
	• Crosses arms over his chest	_____
Feet and legs	• Restless, crosses and uncrosses legs	_____
	• Taps feet, moves feet in awkward manner	_____
Posture	• Rigid	_____
	• Places objects between the two of you	_____
	• Shifts his body constantly	_____
	• Moves away from you when you get close	_____

EXTRA MILEAGE LOG

Step 1:

First, establish "normal" mileage (days you know car is driven to/from work only—no chance of extra miles added)

Date/day of the week of normal mileage

Date _____ Day of the Week _____

Start Odometer _____

Ending Odometer _____

Total Normal Miles _____

Step 2:

Calculate "suspicious" mileage (days you suspect car is driven to meet lover)

Log

Date/day of the week of extra mileage

Date _____ Day of the Week _____

Start Odometer _____

Ending Odometer _____

Total Suspicious Miles_____

Total Normal Miles _____

= Unaccounted for Miles _____

Date/day of the week of extra mileage

Date _____ Day of the Week _____

Start Odometer _____

Ending Odometer _____

Total Suspicious Miles_____

Total Normal Miles _____

= Unaccounted for Miles _____

Date/day of the week of extra mileage

Date _____ Day of the Week _____

Start Odometer _____

Ending Odometer _____

Total Suspicious Miles_____

Total Normal Miles _____

= Unaccounted for Miles _____

SUNDAY	MONDAY	TUESDAY	WEDNESDAY	THURSDAY	FRIDAY	SATURDAY

CHAPTER 4
Affairs Take Work

If your spouse is having an affair, there's a good chance—a very good chance—that it began at work. In fact, the vast majority of affairs are nurtured and maintained in the workplace. Ninety percent of the people whose cases we've worked on place the affair's origin in a work-related environment. Infidelity experts, including therapists, attorneys, and private investigators like ourselves, confirm that the workplace is, in effect, the undisputed leading locale for illicit relationships.

As we noted earlier, no two affairs are identical, so the affair you suspect may not have any relation to your partner's workplace. We of course appreciate the fact that infidelity can begin in any setting, in any situation. If it can take place in the White House, it can occur anywhere—a church, a bridge club, a school, on a cruise, in a hospital—two people can get together. But in reality most affairs blossom from nine to five, and therefore the office remains the prime place to consider when determining if an affair has compromised your relationship.

Why the Workplace Cultivates Affairs

What are the enabling qualities that make the office such a hotbed of affairs? What is it about the nature of the workplace that makes it contribute to or even enhance the odds of an affair's developing? There are many reasons, but by looking at the most important ones, you will gain a clearer understanding of how an affair originates.

When women joined the workforce in increasing numbers beginning soon after World War II, workplace-incubated infidelity skyrocketed. And while this fundamental change has brought massive and lasting advances to our society as a whole, transforming gender roles forever, the one unintended and seminal consequence is the rise in office affairs. The advent of women and men working together in close proximity (often in moderately stressful situations for eight, nine, ten, or more hours a day, week in and week out) has contributed more to the increase in infidelity than any other single societal change. This is not the fault of one gender or the other or of a sudden abandonment of our collective moral scruples. It is simply the result of giving more men and women the opportunity to meet and communicate about work, TV shows, politics, home life, and thus build friendships that all too easily evolve into closer ties, which in turn can lead to an illicit affair.

Consider this: Weekends aside, many of us spend more of our waking hours at work (and commuting to work) than we do at home with our own families. And during those hours at the office, men and women interact on work matters large and small, they share victories and also defeats, they build friendships and confidences. Now, stir together these elements— members of the opposite sex spending hours a day in close proximity, sharing work experiences, developing friendships and bonds. It's not surprising that this potent mixture can result in an affair.

Many people conduct affairs at work for the most obvious reason—their spouse isn't there acting as a countervailing force, keeping them in check. Plus, your absence from your partner's work space allows the out-of-sight, out-of-mind attitude to prevail. *What she doesn't know won't hurt her* is a prevalent rationalization among cheaters. But justifying one's actions, especially unacceptable ones, plays a major role in perpetuating affairs. If it doesn't lend full legitimacy to illicit behavior, it at least sanctions it in the cheater's eyes.

The workplace also fosters the combat-buddy syndrome: Coworkers who are fully aware of an existing office affair and possibly know the wife who is being cheated on often employ a selective morality, choosing not to inform the wife. Of course, *they* would want to know if *their* spouses were running around on them. But different dynamics and ethics govern the office. The "It's their own private business, not mine" attitude rules, trumping the "His wife should know about this" view. Perhaps not surprising, this detached, uninvolved stance in large measure is because of the fact that it's far easier *not* telling than telling and contributing to the inevitable unpleasant consequences. Add to that the reality that most people don't want to see themselves—or be seen by others—as a classic snitch. Of course, many affairs are exposed, or at least verified, with the anonymous phone call or letter to the cheated-on partner. The (almost always anonymous) coworker who serves as the tipster is a rare species. Consequently, with most coworkers who know of an affair refusing to notify the most important person about it, the workplace can become a sort of haven for an affair to continue and even flourish.

The newest advances in technology also make breaking the oldest matrimonial taboo a cinch. If you're old enough to have been working in an office environment twenty or so years ago, odds are that not one of the technological tools that facilitate carrying on an affair today was even around. No call forwarding. No cell phones. No Blackberries. No voicemail. No email. No instant messaging. No text messaging. No computer in every home. No ordering gifts online. No online, actually. These tools that seem indispensable today weren't available a couple of short decades ago—in fact, most were unimaginable back then.

But now lovers at work can quietly send a text message detailing the time and location of where to meet without attracting attention. And that's just one obvious example of how the technologies in today's work space make it easier than ever not only for lovers to communicate their feelings to one another but also manage the logistics of an affair. The instant message has replaced the handwritten love note. Cell phone text messaging has superseded calls from pay phones (which are now relics seen in thirty-year-old movies). As a consequence, the advent of such technologies from the 1980s through today—most of them developed for and first used in the workplace—can realistically be seen as a major development in the evolution of infidelity in modern America, rivaling even the importance of women entering the workforce in the 1950s or the arrival of the birth control pill a decade later.

Signs at Work

Though we've witnessed thousands of affairs and are as familiar with the dynamics, the causes, and the way they play out as anyone could be, we believe that there is no such thing as the typical affair—just as there is no such thing as the typical marriage. Complex relationships driven by the strongest, most deeply felt emotions are each unique, with no two narratives following the same pattern. It's important to keep that in mind as you begin to look at your own relationship, but this time view it through the eyes of a private investigator.

Each and every affair follows its own course, its own rules of behavior. And right now, at this juncture in your relationship, you likely can't control what's going on. That's the reality of it, but it doesn't have to be the future of it. Your job right now is to find out what's happening so you'll know how to begin taking charge of the situation instead of being a pawn in it. What we give you in this chapter and throughout the book are the tools to use in dealing with your specific situation, tools to help you discover what is going on outside your view and for now, outside your control. Here, then, are the key signs to look for with regard to the workplace.

Work Schedule Changes

I always admired Sammy's work ethic. Now ethical is about the last word I'd use.

But, like I said, when we first met, one of the things I liked most about Sammy was how dedicated he was to his career. Look, I never let work get in between us; I knew how important it was to him. Then last summer, I see his work is getting more and more of his time and attention, which meant less of it for me and the kids. In just a matter of weeks, he's going from maybe his regular forty, fifty hours or so a week to like sixty or more, way more. Sure, he's a driven guy, so I believed him when he says "Babe, I'm working late tonight, be home tenish," even though this is on a Friday. But then it's the same thing the next Friday and the next and the next. This isn't right, I thought, especially since he never once called me from the office; too busy, he says. If my friend Hannah hadn't seen Sammy and his cute twenty-three-year-old assistant cuddling at a bar last Friday, I'd still be in the dark. And he'd still be telling me what a hard worker he is.

Gina T.

Spending what most of us would consider an inordinate amount of time at work serves as a key indicator that a partner could be having an affair. On the other hand, your spouse just might be working extra hard. How do you differentiate between an affair and hours genuinely spent at the gristmill?

First, you need to determine that the additional time at work is actually spent at work and exactly when those extra hours are. Is it truly extreme, such as six, eight, or ten more hours a week? Or only a couple of hours a week? Is it frequent—two or more times a week and usually on a Monday and a Friday, or only sporadic with no set pattern, a day here another one there? For example, because lovers often can't see or even speak with each other over the weekend, the days surrounding the weekend—Fridays and Mondays—are often times when the cheating couple arrange to see each other. So if you're noticing that your husband has begun working late virtually every Monday evening or has started to go out for a few drinks with the guys at work almost every Friday, make a note of it. Likewise, if he works late on the same night of the work week, there's a good chance that's the one night that his lover is able to arrange to see him. To aid you in determining if your spouse's additional hours at work or added time spent with work buddies after work fit a pattern that signals something serious, use the Extra Hours Log on p. 85.

Follow the Money (or the Lack of It)

Dougie's making $32.50 an hour, good union job. And now he's working five, six, seven hours a week overtime, and there's no extra money? No way, no how.

Oh, maybe he's working for free, hadn't thought of that one. See why I'm suspicious? After a month of this working late, usually on Mondays and always on Fridays, I see our bank statement and the direct deposit for his paycheck's identical to a month ago, to two months ago, not a penny more. "Whoa," I ask him, "they didn't put in your extra pay?" Dougie hems and he haws and mutters something about dues and extra contributions, and I let it go. But this month it's the same thing! I figure we should be over $700 richer, but now I'm also figuring that Dougie's got a lot of explaining to do.

Barbara K.

Assuming their company pays for overtime, when cheaters say they're working late or going in early, one of the questions to ask is, "Then where's the extra money?" Or if your partner receives the same salary no matter how many hours he works, where's the tangible proof that he's receiving recognition for working all these additional hours? You could ask, "Doesn't your boss say anything about your working all these extra hours?"

and "Does everyone you work with have to work these hours?" We'll show you how to log and gauge the response to this and other questions on the log sheets at the end of this chapter. If you have to even think of asking questions like these, you can assume that something in your partner's behavior has aroused your suspicion—trust your gut instinct.

It's important to note the degree of calmness and sincerity when your partner responds—does he sound defensive, equivocating, or perhaps rattled by the questions? Or do the answers sound credible and believable, delivered quickly without hesitation or a trace of angst or quick temper? Remember, you're dealing with cheating here, so you should expect a good acting performance. But if you know your spouse well enough, there's a good chance you'll be able to distinguish between really having to work late and lying about all those extra hours slaving away at the job. If the answers make you feel apprehensive in their inconclusiveness and evasion, you can rightfully feel suspicious and plan on diligently following as many other signs as possible. As we discussed in the last chapter, you can read your spouse's body language to see if he's telling you the truth or doing his best to hide it from you. The log sheets at the end of this chapter allow you to capture your sense of the sincerity of your partner's responses.

The Days of Our Lies

Tanya and I had a regular card game with friends every Friday night. Then Tanya got herself another friend.

But even before she told me, I figured it out. For ten years at least, we'd meet with Harriet and Burt on Friday nights for bridge, one Friday at their place, the next at ours. Of course we didn't play every Friday but pretty regularly. Then I guess around four or five weeks ago, Tanya calls from her office on Friday, says she has a lot of work and asks me if we can make it a little later. I say sure, and she comes home around 8:30 or so, and off we go to play bridge. The next Friday, same routine, she calls, she's working late, only now she keeps our friends and me waiting, arriving around 9:00, and it was like this for a over a month, always on Friday, always late. Then last week Tanya says she wants a separation so she could "find herself," but I already suspected she was cheating at Hearts.

Howard Y.

Possibly the most important warning sign involves a pattern developing, especially on Fridays and Mondays (as we've said, these are the days before and after the weekend apart from the lover). If this occurs, you should consider that your partner could be meeting a lover before the weekend begins, right after it ends, or both. You should view any day or days when your spouse follows a specific schedule as a potential signal that something other than work could be at play here. We've had clients whose spouses had gambling habits or drug habits that they satisfied on a regular basis—no affair, but *still* a problem. To help track your partner's time at work to determine it there is a problem, use the Extra Hours Log at the end of the chapter.

When Voicemail Answers

Tim complains that he's sick and tired of a desk job. Fine. But how come he's never at his desk when I call at night?

Well now I know why: He wasn't even at work. I sensed something was off with us, he'd been acting stranger and stranger at home, quiet, then getting angry over nothing, and I mean nothing. But I knew there was trouble when I tried to call him to tell him that his uncle was taken to the hospital. That night, a Monday, he was working late again, seemed like every Monday was a late work night these days for Tim. Anyway, I call him at work, no answer, call again, no answer. His cell phone must've been off, 'cause it too went right into voicemail.

Finally, I call the company's main number, get a security guard on the line and say it's a kind of medical emergency and ask if he could please go get Tim. "Ma'am," the nice guard says, "this office is all closed and locked, no one here but me." So when Tim gets home a few hours later, I ask how work was and he shrugs, "Fine." I owe that security guard, big time.

Joan F.

If your spouse is at work, why are your calls being forwarded to voicemail at 8:20 p.m.? And why doesn't he answer his cell phone? While he could occasionally be in a meeting (depending upon his job), he probably won't be in one all the time unless he's preparing for a big business pitch with other coworkers, or some other crunch is occurring at work. But even if that's the case, you should be able to set a time to call and catch up once in a while. You'll want to try reaching him a few times to get a better sense of his whereabouts. When you do call to check up on him, don't leave messages, and be sure to try to hang up before voicemail is activated so there's no record of your call. In case your partner does pick up, always have a legitimate reason to be calling so it doesn't appear that you're monitoring your partner at work—have the reason prepared before you call so you don't sound flustered in case he answers the phone. Keep the questions or reasons for calling innocuous, but still well worth a call. Here are a few good examples of reasons to call that don't sound like you're checking up: Request that he stop at the drug store on the way home to pick up some over-the-counter medication you need, or you could say that you heard a strange sound the last time you drove his car and ask him to be sure to listen for it on the way home, or tell him you can't find some paperwork or bills and wondered if he's seen them.

If you consistently get voicemail in the evenings (when your partner is supposedly working late) but don't get it as

frequently during normal business hours, then you have reason to be suspicious. Of course there might be legitimate reasons why your calls go to voicemail, but in our experience, if a
spouse can't be easily reached on a regular basis, this signals
a high-level warning sign. The Not Picking Up the Phone at
Work page is designed to help you keep track of unanswered
(and, of course, answered) after-hour (and before-hour) calls
at the office. If over a period of two or three weeks most of the
calls you've made went unanswered, you should read this as a
significantly high warning sign.

On the Road Again . . . and Again . . . and Again

Todd took just one trip too many.

*It was right after the holidays, and Todd says he's got to go to the
head office again this month, another important client meeting with
so and so about the such and such deal. That makes five trips there in
nine weeks, and three of them are over a weekend. Hmmm. But Todd
says it's because he plays golf with the sales manager and a customer,
so I'm not all that suspicious. I even give him the benefit of the doubt.
And to prove that I'm a good sport about it, I write him a sweet note,
saying how much I miss him, roll it up like a little scroll, and slip it
into one of his golf shoes so he'll have a sweet surprise message from
me while he's away. I didn't hear from him about the note, but wasn't
bothered, he's not the sentimental type. When he comes home, I ask him
how his golf was, great, great he says. And then as he unpacks, I see
my rolled up note exactly where I placed it. He was playing OK, just
not golf.*

Martha P.

Now your partner's business might call for an increase in
work-related travel. A client needs attention, a competitor is
making inroads in a certain territory, a new employee requires
on-the-site training, whatever. But if a substantial increase in

trips and/or their duration coincides with other key signs such as working extra hours and unaccountable expenses (as we cover in chapter 5), then you should be concerned. To help you track your partner's business travel schedule, use the Taking Business Trips Log sheet at the end of this chapter. Also, try to recall how many business trips he took in the last couple of years, and then compare that estimate to the number of trips you log in now. A dramatic change that doesn't correspond to legitimate demands made by the company serves as a key indicator that something is amiss.

The Name Game

By the end, we couldn't have a conversation about anything without Jay saying her name.

It was Sheryl said this, Sheryl did that, Sheryl, Sheryl, Sheryl. Whatever the topic, it seemed like he'd find a way to weave her into it. Maybe I'm exaggerating a bit now that I know the whole story; perhaps I didn't realize that something's strange when your sixty-year-old husband and grandfather of three keeps talking about his new paralegal, Sheryl, who's younger than his youngest child. Maybe I thought he's just impressed with her since he's had so much trouble with staff, but my suspicions proved not to be so paranoid, not after I found three condoms in the bottom of his briefcase. I had absolutely no problem figuring out who the other woman was—her name had already become a household fixture.

Tillie L.

This may sound counterintuitive, but often a person who is having an affair with a coworker tends to mention the lover's name with growing frequency at home. Many times when we catch a cheating spouse and identify the lover, our client will say the cheating partner had been bringing up the lover's name with some regularity. The reasons an adulterer mentions the lover's name are complex and individualized—it could serve as a disarming tactic to make the suspecting spouse think the person is simply just another coworker. The cheating spouse might get a thrill by mentioning the lover's name in a seemingly innocent context at home, or the cheater might bring up the name to feel close to the lover during the period of separation, especially over a weekend or holiday period. We've had clients describe this syndrome so often that we've come to accept this odd behavior as a viable sign—and so should you.

The New Friends at Work Log sheet at the end of the chapter will help you keep track of when your partner mentions a coworker's name repeatedly and you sense there might be something going on. Though this sign is not as regularly observed as others relating to affairs at the workplace, when it does occur it serves as a reliable indicator that there is something about the person your spouse finds attractive or memorable.

Turning to Dr. Gunzburg: Why Cheaters Are Cheaters

I have been helping couples survive infidelity for over thirty years, and the one most frequent question I'm asked is: "Why do cheaters cheat?" Why, indeed? The truth is, I don't have an answer—I have many answers, and none is simple. That's because people are such confoundedly complex creatures. The reasons people cheat are likewise complicated and varied. But over the years I've found eight broad groups of answers that cover the spectrum of reasons people are unfaithful to their partners.

Here then are my answers, somewhat simplified, to the question that you are likely asking right now: Why? Why do they cheat?

- They think they are unable to satisfy their needs and cravings within their relationship. They harbor a cock-eyed idea that cheating is a logical and understandable solution to their needs. Nothing, of course, could be further from the truth. But truth isn't what concerns them—satisfaction is all that matters to them.

• They do it because the idea of boundaries is either alien to them or doesn't concern them one whit. Sure they know what boundaries are about, but boundaries are not a part of their world, and so they satisfy their own needs without considering ordinary boundaries of propriety.

• They just love the excitement and thrill of it and it rejuvenates and spurs them on. Cheating being a taboo has the opposite effect on these people than on the rest of us. They are energized and motivated by the taboo of sex outside marriage.

• Male cheaters feel they are incomplete and a failure at being a man if they don't accept a woman's offer of sex; it would mark them as less of a man, less virile and masculine if they walked away from sex with another woman.

• Their extremely low self-esteem compels them to venture outside their marriage for sex. These people think that because the other person with some special characteristic (beauty, wealth, intelligence, power) cares for them, their self-image is elevated.

• Their spouses are unwilling to satisfy their often strange sexual fetishes and demands, and these people find a solution to this by having illicit sex with more willing partners. This often appears when the cheater is at an age where you would expect him to be fully mature. These cheaters are almost always male.

• They have little or no personal scruples and just take any opportunity to have sex. This is similar to the "being a man" answer, but these people don't need any reason except that the sex is available.

- They believe, whether true or not, that their own partners no longer have the capacity or the willingness to
  make them feel desired or special as a sexual partner,
  so they find others who in their eyes do make them feel
  appreciated and desirable.

Varied as these reasons are, there are overarching and related
reasons cheaters do what they do: Cheating is either their
misguided way of arriving at a solution to some problem that
plagues them, or it satisfies some unfulfilled need in their
character and makeup. Furthermore, many cheaters, but not
all, have a warped or highly selective idea of what commitment
means—they feel it really needn't be applied to anything to do
with women. I think chauvinistic is even too gentle a word to
capture how these men view the world, but it certainly is at the
essence of their thinking.

Many of my patients ask why people cheat because they
feel that if they knew the answer they might gain an understanding of how to keep it from repeating. But the fact is, you
really don't need to explore the depths of its origins or all the
possible motivations, because there's no guarantee at all—and
I know this from treating thousands of patients—that having
this information will not thwart future episodes. What keeps a
couple from experiencing the repeat of infidelity is their desire
to survive infidelity together and apply much hard work to
achieve that goal, and that the cheater recognizes a problem in
his character and develops a strong desire to repair his character. He has to want to be the person who could never cheat
on his spouse. So I suggest to my patients that they not obsess
over the question of why it happened; holding on to the question keeps them from moving forward.

As you see, there is no short, simple answer to why people
cheat. But infidelity is not a simple issue to deal with either.
Yet, in *Warning Signs*, I apply much of the knowledge and

insights I use in my practice every day and have put into my books for couples who have been affected by infidelity. This information will help *you* better understand ways to grapple with the trauma of infidelity and survive its consequences.

Workplace Warnings: What to Look For

More than any other single locale or environment, the workplace is where an affair is born. And it's been this way for at least the past fifty years, since the time that women's numbers and job opportunities (though not their wages!) in the office workforce began to match those of men. Of course, affairs can begin and be carried on anywhere—a president of the United States and an intern in the White House proved that point. Because women and men work closely together in often stressful and emotional situations, the chances for a couple to come together are enhanced in a work environment. Also, modern technology, from Blackberries to text messaging, make the logistics and scheming needed to have an office affair far easier than in times past. And the culture of the workplace often makes it unlikely that office workers will inform on their coworkers either by telling upper management or the spouses, should they know them. So if you suspect your husband is having an affair, there's a good chance that the first warning signs of that possibility could be work related, and the most important Workplace Warning signs to look for include:

- A change in his work schedule
- Works more hours
- Leaves for work earlier, stays later
- Additional hours often logged on Mondays and Fridays
- Or, additional hours always on the same day or days of the week

- Despite the added hours, no increase in overtime pay or recognition
- Does not regularly answer his office phone or cell phone on days that he's working late
- Takes more frequent and possibly longer business trips
- Mentions the name of a female coworker with some frequency

The log sheets on pp. 85–90 are designed to help you easily and accurately keep track of these workplace warning signs. As with all log sheets, try to keep them as current as possible—as soon as a clue becomes apparent, write it down so it won't be overlooked or the details won't be forgotten or misstated. As fertile as the workplace can be as a source of warning signs, another category of signs can prove to be of great value—and that's how he spends his income from his workplace on paying for his affair. So let's move on to how to read the monetary warning signs of an affair.

EXTRA HOURS LOG

Date/day of the week of extra work

Date _____ Day of the week _____

Length of extra work _____

Reason for extra work _____

Time home from extra work_____

Date/day of the week of extra work

Date _____ Day of the week _____

Length of extra work _____

Reason for extra work _____

Time home from extra work_____

Date/day of the week of extra work

Date _____ Day of the week _____

Length of extra work _____

Reason for extra work _____

Time home from extra work_____

Date/day of the week of extra work

Date _____ Day of the week _____

Length of extra work _____

Reason for extra work _____

Time home from extra work_____

Date/day of the week of extra work

Date _____ Day of the week _____

Length of extra work _____

Reason for extra work _____

Time home from extra work_____

Date/day of the week of extra work

Date _____ Day of the week _____

Length of extra work _____

Reason for extra work _____

Time home from extra work_____

QUESTIONS TO ASK YOUR SPOUSE ABOUT WORKING EXTRA HOURS

1.

Date _____

Q: Are you being compensated for all of this recent overtime work?

A: _____

_____

2.

Date _____

Q: Has your boss/supervisor noticed that you're working a lot of overtime?

A: _____

_____

3.

Date _____

Q: Because of the overtime you're working, you think you'll be able to get a bonus or a promotion?

A: _____

_____

4.

Date _____

Q: Does anyone else at work have to put in so many extra hours?

A: _____

_____

LEAVING HOME FOR WORK EARLY LOG

Date/day of the week/departure time

Date _____ Day of the week _____

Time _____

Reason for leaving early_____

Date/day of the week/departure time

Date _____ Day of the week _____

Time _____

Reason for leaving early_____

Date/day of the week/departure time

Date _____ Day of the week _____

Time _____

Reason for leaving early_____

Date/day of the week/departure time

Date _____ Day of the week _____

Time _____

Reason for leaving early_____

Date/day of the week/departure time

Date _____ Day of the week _____

Time _____

Reason for leaving early_____

Date/day of the week/departure time

Date _____ Day of the week _____

Time _____

Reason for leaving early_____

NOT PICKING UP THE PHONE AT WORK LOG

Date _____ Day of the week _____
Time _____

Date _____ Day of the week _____
Time _____

Date _____ Day of the week _____
Time _____

Date _____ Day of the week _____
Time _____

Date _____ Day of the week _____
Time _____

Date _____ Day of the week _____
Time _____

Date _____ Day of the week _____
Time _____

Date _____ Day of the week _____
Time _____

TAKING BUSINESS TRIPS LOG

Departure date/day of the week for the trip departure

Date _____ Day of the week _____

Destination/Reason _____

Return date/day of the week

Return date _____ Day of the week _____

Departure date/day of the week for the trip departure

Date _____ Day of the week _____

Destination/Reason _____

Return date/day of the week

Return date _____ Day of the week _____

Departure date/day of the week for the trip departure

Date _____ Day of the week _____

Destination/Reason _____

Return date/day of the week

Return date _____ Day of the week _____

Departure date/day of the week for the trip departure

Date _____ Day of the week _____

Destination/Reason _____

Return date/day of the week

Return date _____ Day of the week _____

NEW FRIENDS AT WORK LOG

Date/day of the week of new friend's name being mentioned

Date _____ Day of the week _____

Name of new friend _____

Reason/context for mentioning the new friend's name _____

_____

Date/day of the week of new friend's name being mentioned

Date _____ Day of the week _____

Name of new friend _____

Reason/context for mentioning the new friend's name _____

_____

Date/day of the week of new friend's name being mentioned

Date _____ Day of the week _____

Name of new friend _____

Reason/context for mentioning the new friend's name _____

_____

Date/day of the week of new friend's name being mentioned

Date _____ Day of the week _____

Name of new friend _____

Reason/context for mentioning the new friend's name _____

_____

Date/day of the week of new friend's name being mentioned

Date _____ Day of the week _____

Name of new friend _____

Reason/context for mentioning the new friend's name _____

_____

Date/day of the week of new friend's name being mentioned

Date _____ Day of the week _____

Name of new friend _____

Reason/context for mentioning the new friend's name _____

_____

SUNDAY	MONDAY	TUESDAY	WEDNESDAY	THURSDAY	FRIDAY	SATURDAY

Use this calendar to determine if there is a pattern to the actions you have logged.

CHAPTER 5
Affairs Don't Come Cheap

The emotional costs of infidelity are incalculable; you can't assign a dollar amount to the broken trust, shattered respect, and devastated family bonds. But there are the actual dollar costs involved in maintaining an affair—costs that can be direct and irrefutable proof that an affair is going on—costs and expenses that you can uncover and document.

Now most cheaters do whatever they can to prevent their own spouses from seeing that they have spent a single penny on the affair. Of course, cheaters try to hide records of money spent at restaurants and bars, hotels and motels, clothing stores and flower shops that could point to the affair. But most times, cheaters can't hide *every* transaction from the eyes of someone, such as you, who is looking for the truth. Somewhere in the cheater's desk, in his wallet, bureau drawer, briefcase, or even pants pockets lies a credit card or cash receipts not meant for your eyes—and these items are being kept from your view for only one reason: They prove that an affair is going on.

To Catch a Cheater You Can't Get Caught Yourself

Let's say you have every right to suspect your partner of infidelity; he's been logging ever-increasing hours at work, or he's joined a gym and is wearing an all-new wardrobe. Despite your suspicions—or actually *because* of them—you have to take every precaution you can to keep well-founded speculation from becoming reciprocated. You do *not* want your cheating spouse to get wind of your quest for the truth and begin questioning *your* behavior. So, as you learned in chapter one, the best sleuths are the ones who don't let on to anyone, especially their partner, that they are indeed investigating.

How do you keep your spouse from discovering that you're looking for financial proof of an affair? The best tactic is to make him feel more confident that you have absolutely no clue at all, that you're not entertaining the least amount of suspicion or concern. We've designed the following guidelines to help minimize your spouse's discovering that you're on to the possibility that something, and someone, has come on the scene.

The What, When, Where, and How of Chasing the Money

During the early investigations into the Watergate scandal, newspaper reporters Bob Woodward and Carl Bernstein received very fertile advice from the White House source they code-named Deep Throat. "Follow the money," he told them, and indeed that is how the two sleuthing reporters were able to track payments made to the Watergate burglars all the way back to the White House. The rest is, of course, history, but "follow the money" has as much currency today as ever. What that famous phrase implies is that money talks, and it speaks not just in the power it conveys, but in your case it can inform you rather conclusively of an affair. Once your partner has spent money, a paper trail often remains in the form of receipts, invoices, statements, expense forms—essentially anything and everything that records a sales transaction.

Because we are creatures of habit, we tend to follow routines, practices, and ways to handle the regular events and chores in our lives. Most of us retain receipts for larger expenses while tossing the receipts for the shampoo and toothpaste we picked up at the drugstore on the way home from work. But a $65 dinner tab, especially if it's paid with a credit or debit card, is likely to be somewhere. It's your job to find out where that somewhere is—and we'll show you how.

But, you might ask, what if he's paying for this suspected affair primarily with cash? Shouldn't that make following the money trail an impossible task? No, not impossible—more difficult, yes, but certainly not impossible. One of the greatest advances in consumer banking in the last quarter century is the now ubiquitous and seemingly indispensable cash-dispensing ATM. We still remember standing in line at the bank to get cash from our own bank account—hard to imagine these days. But besides handing us our cash whenever and almost wherever we want, the ATM also gives us a complete record of each transaction—how much was withdrawn and where. This means the bank statement can clearly show you how much cash he's taking out, when he's doing it, and even from what part of town. By comparing cash withdrawals over a period of, say, ten or twelve months, you should be able to see an increasing amount of total cash withdrawn. Let's say the total average withdrawn over a twelve-month time frame is $600 a month, but starting three or four months ago, the average withdrawn was $800 or $900 a month. That money is going for an extra expense, or else there'd be no need to withdraw more on a steady basis.

Note the days of the withdrawals—do they coincide with days and evenings when your partner is supposedly working late? (This is another reason to keep the Extra Hours Log sheet presented in chapter 4.) If, for example, your partner withdraws something like $50 or $100 in cash every Thursday morning and works late every Thursday evening, it's probably not a coincidence—he could be using the funds to pay for a dinner, a motel room, or both. But before you jump to conclusions, you need to see a defined, repeatable pattern developing, not just a random withdrawal that's somewhat higher than usual. If he's paying for the affair on a mostly cash-only basis, you'll be able to see evidence of that in the increase in frequency and in the size of the cash withdrawals. So if you find that your partner takes out a meaningful amount of cash every week, week after week (that is greater than normal), and there's no logical reason why, then you've got more than enough reason to be alarmed.

Also, try to calculate if your partner appears to spend less money in other areas to cover the costs of his having an affair. An affair takes an investment of time and money (not to mention the emotional investment). Money in most households is finite, as very few of us have a bottomless pit of financial resources. Your household probably resembles most others, with just so much money to spend every month. Your expenses, including those for dining out and entertainment/gifts (let's call them the semiluxuries of our lives), remain the same every month, more or less. If that sounds like your situation, then use the Comparison of Expenditures Log on p. 114 to do a rough evaluation; add up the number of times and the amount spent on those semiluxuries such as dining out, going to movies or clubs, and gifts today versus, say, six months ago or before you think the possible affair really began.

For example, if you and your spouse consistently dined out an average of two to three times a week about a year ago, and now you're dining out just once or twice a week, then there's a chance that some of the funds he once allocated to dining out with you have shifted to cover his ongoing expenses for an affair. Of course he might claim that he's just too busy working late to dine out with you. No matter what the excuse, log any decrease in the number of times dining out or going to a movie or whatever form of out-of-home entertainment you used to enjoy BTA (before the affair).

Having an Affair Really Does Make a Statement

Chances are, cold cash isn't the only way your partner is funding the illicit relationship. Much of the expense—for dinners, for gifts, for motels—could be charged to his personal business credit card or debit card. Unless your partner wants to get caught, it's highly unlikely those charges are going to appear on a charge card statement the two of you share, though you should carefully peruse the credit card statements for shared cards, making note of suspicious charges. Do *not* make notes on the actual statement itself, as you don't want your partner to see that you've been examining his or your joint charge card statements. Instead, use the Unexplained/Suspicious Purchases Log sheet at the end of this chapter.

If your spouse personally receives monthly charge card statements, and he's the one who regularly opens the statement envelopes, do not be tempted to open them yourself, as it may inform him of your suspicions. Is there a file where your partner keeps the credit card statements? If so, it could be a potential gold mine of evidence but one that you need to approach carefully, without leaving any signs that indicate you're mining for clues. Look at the statements *only* when there's virtually no chance that you'll be caught. Here, too, either make copies or write down every suspicious charge. And look back at least a year or longer if you suspect the affair has gone on a good while.

So, there they are, the credit card statements, all tucked away. Let's say they're in a file in his home office desk. Now that you've found them, what charges should you make special notice of?

Restaurants

Eating what must be fifty dinners alone at home isn't the only thing that's eating me these days.

Donny was working late a lot, or so he told me, but often would come home from those late nights smelling of breath mints and booze. The few times I asked if he'd had a drink, he'd say I was imagining it, so I wouldn't push it as he was already getting testy enough. Then in getting papers for our tax accountant, I see a bunch of charges over the last four or five months at Roma's, an Italian place on the other side of town. We, as in Donny and me, haven't eaten there in years, years! But he sure has. So when Donny gets home that night, I say, "You know, I'd like to have dinner this Saturday at that place we used to go to, you know, Roma's?" Donny's face turns as red as marinara sauce.

Meg G.

Because most affairs are inherently clandestine, the lovers have to meet in places their own friends, family members, coworkers, and associates don't frequent. Look for charges made at eating establishments located far from where your partner works or where you live. And if you do find suspicious expenses, be sure to log the date of the charge to see if it coincides with the dates of the "extra" work hours. Also, because lovers tend to have one or two favorite places to share their romantic dinners, search for charges made at the same restaurant, week after week, often on the same day of the week. One caveat: The charge date on the printed statement may be two, three, or more days later than the actual charge, which can be because the establishment reported the charge after the actual date of purchase.

Hotels

In his briefcase I find a letter from Marriott hotels congratulating him on becoming a rewards member. Odd, considering he hasn't left Phoenix in nine months.

I wasn't snooping, just looking for his business card to give to a neighbor whose husband's company was looking for an IT consultant. I reach in and here's this rewards member letter. Something doesn't make sense—I mean, Clay hasn't traveled in months, let alone checked into a hotel. So every morning when he's in the shower, I go through his briefcase, and on the fourth or fifth day, bingo, I find his credit card statement showing that a month ago he had five stays at the Marriott on Camelback—right here in Phoenix! This is the reward I get for being a loyal wife?

Sharon K.

You don't need experienced private detectives like us to tell you that if you find charges made at motels and hotels that do not appear to be related to any business trip (they're for hotels right in your town!), you've found the most blatantly obvious sign that he's in the midst of an affair. In case this happens, try to remain as calm as possible—don't take the copy of the receipt to confront your partner the minute he steps through the front door. Instead, tell yourself to stay cool and collected; you're on a mission to get the facts. So log each suspicious motel or hotel expense and continue your job of gathering all the evidence you can. For example, use the blank calendar at the end of this chapter to place each charge and activity in the day of the week each occurred. This way you'll see if the restaurant charges coincide with any motel and hotel charges; if you do find some, that's clearly additional proof. The point is, you want to build as solid a case as you can, with as much information as possible so that it will be futile for him to deny the affair.

We've had cases where credit card statements detailed dozens of nonbusiness-related hotel stays at a time when the spouse was in town—and not surprisingly those dates often coincided with restaurant purchases. Perhaps the cheating spouse thought his partner would never think of looking at the charge card statement. But cheaters often will either try to hide or even destroy a credit card statement that month after month is filled with so many suspicious charges. To further shield themselves from getting caught, many cheating spouses will acquire a new credit card, unbeknownst to the spouse, to pay for the motel and hotel charges for their trysts, using their office address as the billing address. But by searching the wastebasket, wallet and briefcase (which we'll discuss later in this chapter), you might be able to locate evidence of charges made to a secret charge card. And in the next chapter, you'll learn where to acquire computer spyware that enables you to capture charge card payments he might have made online using his home office computer.

Clothes

I'm checking Jack's suit coat pockets before taking in the dry cleaning and find a charge card receipt from two weeks ago for a scarf bought at Nanette's. I'm still waiting for the gift.

And I know it'll never come—because the scarf was obviously for Jack's lover. I didn't tell him what I found, I just keep collecting other clues, like his having a lot more late dinners with "clients," his moodiness at home, and his sudden new penchant for designer shirts, even though the shirt buttons around his belly are about to burst. Amazing what a little slip of paper can lead to.

Andrea E.

As you learned in chapter 2, one important sign of a partner's cheating is the appearance of new, often more expensive and even slightly showier and more stylish clothing. Those credit card charges are not the ones you're looking for, because the items he bought are hanging in his clothes closet, not hidden away from you. But there are clothes charges you do need to look for, charges for clothes that *aren't* hanging in his closet but in someone else's. Namely, his lover's. So look for apparel charges for the other gender— the only reason a man would buy a woman's scarf or sweater, or a woman would be buying a man's tie or shirt is to give it as a gift. And if you've noticed that you certainly haven't been unwrapping any gifts from him lately, then he probably made those purchases for his lover.

Jewelry

"Shellie," I ask, "where'd you get that bracelet?" She says, "At a tag sale, I didn't tell you?" Yeah, sure, maybe at a Beverly Hills tag sale.

I'm no jeweler, but this isn't like the costume jewelry you see sitting on a card table in front of someone's house. Some guy spent a lot on it. I just hope the guy's wife finds out that her husband has very good taste in jewelry, especially when it comes to pieces not intended for her. In the meantime, I told Shellie that the tag game's over.

Joe S.

More often than not, the man buys jewelry for his lover—but a woman too can buy her lover a bracelet or a neck chain. A gift of jewelry, usually but not always, signals that the affair has been going on for a while; because of its high cost and personal appeal (who doesn't like jewelry?), lovers often give each other jewelry for special dates such as birthdays and anniversaries, perhaps their six-month anniversary of the beginning of the affair. Even if the gift wasn't given in recognition of a specific date, the fact that such an expensive and personal gift was given at all is a sign of the intensity and possibly the length of the affair. So if you do find credit card charges for jewelry, even just one or two, you should see this as all the more reason to examine credit card statements for the other indicators.

Business Trips

I couldn't believe the amount of the hotel charges on Craig's receipts. In fact, I couldn't believe anything about the trip.

I got a call from Craig's office, someone in personnel, sorry he's calling Craig at home when he's taking a personal day, but they have a question about a new hire and . . . huh? Personal day? I say he's not taking a personal day, he's in Sacramento on a one-day business trip. The guy sounds confused and hangs up. So when Craig gets back that night I say nothing, but when he's in the shower, I go through his suitcase, then his attaché, and that's where I find a receipt from a hotel in Lake Tahoe with a room service charge of $146! For one person? For one night? I think I might be doing some traveling of my own.

Ellen Ruth F.

A few years ago we read about one of the most famous marketing blunders in history, one that we really identified with. It's also one that points out the need to check your partner's travel expense reports and credit card statements. Back in the 1960s, a large national airline wanted to build customer loyalty with its lucrative business-class clientele. So the airline came up with a promotion offering the business traveler (who back then was almost exclusively male) the opportunity to take his wife along on the trip for a fraction of the regular price. All that the business traveler had to do was register his wife's name and home address. After the short promotion was over, the airline's marketing geniuses sent a thank-you letter to all the lucky wives of the business travelers, telling them how much the airline appreciated their flying with them and that they hoped they had an enjoyable trip. Many of the wives receiving the letter had the identical reaction: *Trip? What trip?!* You can imagine the trauma and lasting impact this otherwise innocent and innocuous letter brought to many households. This also might explain why for years afterward few offers like this one were made by airlines.

That marketing debacle points out one of the most popular methods lovers use to spend extended time together—a "business trip." In fact, many times the business trip has absolutely nothing to do with business, as the partner merely takes off a day or two and flies or drives off with his lover while his wife thinks he's on a legitimate business trip. If you look carefully at the charges made during your spouse's business trips, you might find the motel or hotel bill is quite high for a single guest, because of ordering room service for two that might include a romantic dinner complete with a bottle of bubbly. So if the hotel charges seem high for a hardworking person traveling alone, he might not have been working hard, or been alone, either.

Second Cell Phone

The movie's about to start, Candice turns off her cell phone, then I see her reach further into her bag and turn off a second phone. What?

I don't say anything, but I couldn't even concentrate on the movie. Afterward, I ask what's up with the new phone. Candice turns white, says it's from the office, an emergency phone for emergency calls in case she loses her phone. Oh, an auto parts supply company must have big emergencies all the time. Who is she fooling, and who is she fooling around with? I told her we have a lot to talk about.

Warren P.

In chapter 6 you'll learn how to use his cell phone statement and the actual cell phone to find out if he's calling one person with far greater frequency than other people. But the cell phone charges we're talking about here deal with not just a new phone number that's showing up but an entire cell phone. To avoid having their suspecting partners find their cell phone record of calls, cheaters use a clever yet expensive tactic of buying a separate cell phone just for the use of making and receiving calls from their lover.

While you'll likely never see or hear your partner on his "lovers' line," you might be able to verify its existence. Again, it's often the male lover who's buying this kind of expensive item because he probably has more disposable income to cover an expense like this. So if you find a charge for the purchase of a new cell phone account (look for this initial purchase charge, as it will likely be made on a credit card—the subsequent monthly billing will probably be sent to his office), you can be almost certain that phone was bought for use in furthering the affair.

Viagra

I give Donny credit for getting Viagra to help with his problem. But now we have a much more serious problem.

Back in the fall, after Donny's doctor prescribed Viagra, our sex lives improved, really did. But the affection wasn't there, not like before, not like the Donny I've been married to for twenty-two years. But I thought, it's a phase, it'll pass. Then a couple of weeks ago, I'm looking in his medicine cabinet to see if he needs more blades, and there's a new bottle of Viagra, but the label is from a Canadian pharmacy, which seems odd. So I go check his file of credit card statements in our office, find the recent pharmacy charges OK, but they're for three refills, all in one shipment. So where are the other bottles? Something's up, and I'm not talking about what Viagra's prescribed for.

Sybil M.

The greatest impetus of an affair can be sex. The illicit character of the affair, with its clandestine encounters in out-of-the-way bars and restaurants, coded text messages, and surreptitious conversations in the office stairwell all add drama, tension, and passion to an affair, making the sexual component even more exciting and fulfilling. And in the past eight or nine years, we've seen a new way that couples in an affair have found to further enhance and continue that heightened sense of sexual passion that dominated their relationship at its inception: Welcome to the world of Viagra.

Perhaps, not surprisingly, women in illicit affairs can purchase Viagra for they certainly benefit from this now-renowned sexual performance-enhancing drug. In many cases, of course, the wife is well aware that the husband takes Viagra, but only later does she learn that the first prescription for it roughly corresponds with the beginning of the affair. And talk about adding insult to injury: We've even had male clients who discovered that their wives were giving their husband's Viagra to their own lovers.

Often the purchases of Viagra are conducted over the Internet (and/or using Canadian "pharmacies"), so look for charges made to companies that have names that often include "drugs" and "drugstore" in them.

Flowers and Other Gifts

Roses are red, and now he knows his florist receipts are read too.

 It all happened because I left my laptop at the office. I asked Rod if I could use his home office computer for a couple minutes to check my email—I never use his, it's a PC and I'm an Apple person, you know what I mean. He says sure, I log on to my account, but as I'm doing that, I see a file marked "Online Receipts" and my curiosity gets the better of me. I click on it, and there's a list of his online purchases— office supplies, the cat food, and, oh look, there's one from Teleflora.com. Teleflora.com? Who'd he buy flowers for? Not me. The receipt shows the date, amount, and the name of a woman Rob works with. I print it out, close the files, and he doesn't know yet what I know. But he will, and he'll need more than flowers to fix this.

Helen G.

Illicit love blooms eternal, which is why we find so many charges to florists made by cheaters. Because cut flowers are perishable and can easily be delivered to the lover's workplace (where they will never be seen by a spouse), they are very popular gifts often given by the man in the affair. Flowers are almost always charged, so look for charges to well-known online florists (1800Flowers.com and Teleflora.com, for example) and to local flower shops as well.

 Flowers are often sent to a lover after a fight or some dramatic episode in the affair, so there's usually no relation between the date of the purchase and a recent holiday, for example. But if you find a charge for flowers (and you haven't been the recipient of a bunch of long-stemmed roses in the last few weeks), you can regard that as a very high-level warning sign.

 Smaller purchases of gifts (other than jewelry and clothes) are difficult to locate, as gift shops often have peculiar, idiosyncratic names so the store's name can be either misleading or unfamiliar to you. But add each and every purchase that is unaccountable to the Unexplained/Suspicious Purchases Log at the end of this chapter, including the cost, date of purchase, and the item, if stated.

The Blatant and Not So Blatant: Individual Receipts

Bank and credit card statements can display a full picture of all the purchases and charges over a period of time. We liken it to a novel with a narrative story, as you can sometimes trace the trajectory of the affair over a month. But individual receipts are more like snippets or scenes in that book. Any receipt you find, no matter where you find it—at the bottom of a waste-basket, tucked away in a wallet, or in an envelope stuffed with sundry receipts—can have important information. Look for these key elements to log: the establishment where the purchase was made, the precise item sold, the date and time of the transaction, and the cost. The Unexplained/Suspicious Purchases Log at the end of the chapter is designed to let you fill in all these elements, along with an adjacent "Reason/Excuse" section if there's something markedly special or worth recording about a particular purchase—for example, if the date of the restaurant receipt corresponds with the date of a motel bill on a charge card statement.

Unlike searching through bank and credit card statements, which you can usually locate easily in your home office or filing cabinet, finding actual receipts can require a bit more digging. Start paying more attention to the papers in your partner's garbage pail, slips of paper in his jacket pockets, or the bunch of receipts hastily stashed in his wallet (when you can get your hands on it). Everyone gets careless sometimes, and the more alert you are to the little clues, the more likely you will uncover something your partner recklessly left where you could find it.

Trash

Let's talk trash now. By that we mean the paper trail you might find in the wastebasket—it can speak volumes! In fact in most states evidence gathered from trash can be admissible in court (as long as it meets other standards for evidence). At this stage, of course, you're simply looking for signs of an affair. But just in case you think that going through the trash is beneath you, consider this: Betraying your trust is far worse than anything you can do to find the truth, including combing through the trash to uncover the facts you need.

One of the best things about doing such an unimaginable act is precisely the fact that it *is* almost unimaginable—your spouse is highly unlikely to consider that you'd do such a thing, which means there could be a reasonably good chance that your garbage hunt will yield fruitful results. So when he's not around, comb through the wastebaskets he uses, especially ones used for paperwork, such as a wastebasket next to the computer or in the home office area. You're looking for any receipts, bills, statements, and while you're at it, scraps of paper with notes and/or phone numbers scribbled on them. You can keep all this "tossed" evidence, unlike the statements or receipts you might find in a file, which should not be removed lest he suspect you're suspicious. And be sure to keep the pilfered-from-the-waste evidence in a secure, hidden place so he won't accidentally stumble upon it.

Of course, the reality is that your cheating spouse might know how reckless it would be to cavalierly toss yesterday's motel receipt into the wastebasket next to his home computer. But you never know. So it's well worth your taking the time and trouble to conduct the unpleasant but possibly highly rewarding task of checking the trash for hard-copy signs of an affair.

Wallet or Briefcase

A plethora of information can be held in a wallet or briefcase (or backpack, if he uses one). You should open his wallet or check his briefcase only when he's absolutely not going to walk in on you (when he's in the shower, dozing, or out of the house) for receipts, statements, and other signs of purchases. Specifically look for small charge card receipts from restaurant purchases, as they are often tucked away in a wallet. A briefcase can be a treasure trove of receipts and statements, because he might feel safer carrying them around rather than leaving them at home or at the office.

It Doesn't Have to Deal with Money to Be a Valuable Find

Besides credit card statements and cash receipts, look for notes scribbled on scraps of paper with an unknown phone number or address (usually without a person's name attached to it), a name of a restaurant, bar, or motel, or any business's name that he would be carrying around because it might be useful in helping him carry on the affair. Be especially attuned to scraps of paper with notes, numbers, or information written in another person's hand, likely a woman's handwriting. If your partner smokes, pay attention to any matchbooks from bars or restaurants you've never heard of or visited—if the matchbooks were hardly used but tossed into the trash, that's a sign that he doesn't want to keep them, as they could be linked to an establishment where the lovers meet.

Turning to Dr. Gunzburg: How Much Do You Really Need to Know? (The Costs, and the Value, of Finding Out Everything)

Let's say that you followed Tony and Dawn's excellent advice and tips, such as finding expense records that offer incontrovertible proof showing, without doubt, that you've been cheated on. Amazing as it may seem, quite a few cheaters deny the affair even with the evidence staring them in the face. At some point, though, if you are persistent, your partner has no choice but to admit to it. After the initial shock and trauma, you arrive at a stage where you need to know about the affair, you think you absolutely have to hear the details, the facts, the whole picture. In short, you want to talk about the affair, not about you and your partner, not about your future yet, and not about your relationship in the past but about the *affair*. This is totally understandable, completely expected, and fraught with danger. Let's say your husband is willing to talk about the affair with you because he wants to move the healing process along as much as you do. Even with a willing partner, you should think about what you want to know.

Questions that pose comparisons between you and the lover are risky ones. These can be far more detrimental than helpful if the answers might leave you with a legend you can never stand up to. Early on after the revelation of the affair, your spouse might still be harboring angry feelings toward you, and as a result, may make his response a hurtful one. An affair is based on fantasy. Any comparison is the real you with your faults magnified versus the fantasized paramour with positive characteristics magnified. If you feel you truly can't get to the next level until you have a question-and-answer session dedicated to the affair itself, then go ahead, but with care. Here are the kinds of questions I most frequently hear asked by the person who's been injured:

- Just what does she offer that I don't offer?
- What are the things she does that I could do too?
- What kinds of things did the two of you do together? (I am thinking I want to make sure you and I never do those things or go to those places.)
- Compared to me, how'd you treat her differently? And the same?
- Are there things you said and did with her that you and I never did together?
- Since you obviously told her things about me and us, don't you think you should reciprocate and tell me things about you and her?
- Were you a better lover with her than you are or were with me?

- Be honest—just how much did you really love her?
- Tell me, if she asked you would you leave me for her?
- How did the thing end? Are you here because I'm the only one of us who still wants you?
- What was your last communication of any kind with your lover?

Of course, you'll probably have your own specific questions to add to or to substitute for the ones I presented here. What I've found to be helpful is to carefully consider your questions one by one and write each one down, then put your list away out of sight, say, in a book, and leave it there for a few days. Then return to your list and reconsider each question and its worst-possible answer. If after this consideration you feel you want to ask your questions, then do. Your spouse has the opportunity to begin bridging the gap between you by answering openly and honestly. Don't expect this to be completed in one session. And expect this to be difficult for each of you. It won't be easy, it won't be painless, and it won't be totally constructive. But it holds the opportunity to move you both to a higher level of awareness and healing.

The Rules of Engagement

If your partner agrees, albeit reluctantly, to discuss the affair, I have some guidelines to recommend. Remember, you're asking questions to help the healing of yourself and your marriage. Your cheating spouse has this opportunity to put down a building block toward rebuilding trust by answering your questions as fully as possible, and of course with complete honesty.

- You, the injured party, should be the one in charge of the questioning and the conversation so you can manage what you can and want to handle.

- Your cheating spouse might warn you about a minefield and suggest you don't want to go there. You can make the decision step by step, feeling your way along the information path that only your spouse knows.
- Honesty rules here. And that's a particularly good thing for the cheater, for he is expected to be totally honest and tell the whole truth. But he's not to use this as a forum to be brutal in the name of honesty.
- As the adage says, be careful what you wish for. You might be hoping to learn everything, and some of what you learn might be extremely distressful. You don't have to do everything in one session. You can take a break, create a new list of questions, and go through the thinking-out process over several days or several weeks before you have another session.
- And as I said earlier, steer away from questions that focus on comparing you and the lover, especially questions dealing with sexual issues or looks. These questions almost never produce information of any value because there is no level playing field where the two of you can be compared—you're real and the lover is not. Sure the lover was a real person, but the rendezvous were just for having fun—not the world most couples live in. There are bills, and children, and other obligations. These unfair comparisons almost always cause more distress and are not worth asking.

As helpful as this question-and-answer session dealing with the affair can be, it is still only one of the numerous ways healing can begin for the individual and for the couple. It will help you to work on your pain, and it could provide your partner with the chance to prove his willingness to be honest and forthright. And in doing so, it will serve as a meaningful tool to begin to put the affair behind you.

Money Talks

Affairs are driven by passion and personal needs while testing the emotional fortitude of the affected spouse and family. But some of the most important and useful warning signs are cold, unfeeling, impersonal numbers in the form of expenditures and dates that show how and where a suspected cheater spends his money. These facts can prove not just whether he's having an affair but also provide you with important details such as where and how often the lovers meet and even illuminate the nature and depth of the affair.

How to Follow the Money

As clever as cheaters can be, they can't conceal every clue. This is especially true when it comes to hiding how they're paying for an illicit relationship. So, following the trail of the money can prove to be a most worthwhile path to take. But while you're on it, be very careful to cover your tracks and not let him sense that you're looking at anything and everything you can find that shows how and where he's spending his money.

What to look for:

1. ATM withdrawals, which indicate he's paying for the affair partially or totally with cash
   a. Higher average amounts withdrawn now than previously
   b. Withdrawals on the same day of the week coinciding with "working late" dates or other clues

2. Decreased expenditures in other areas (such as dining out with you) indicating he's using the money to fund an affair

3. Bank and credit card statements (if you have access or can gain access to them)

a. Photocopy if possible or notes on separate sheets

b. No sign or indication statements have been touched

4. What to look for on the statements (review for at least six months or a year for new kinds of expenses):

a. Information on restaurants

   i. Location—not close to home or to his office

   ii. Date—on same days as "working late"?

   iii. Frequency—same place(s), same day of the week

b. Information on hotels

   i. Location—in your town or nearby?

   ii. Date—on the same days as other clues?

c. Information on clothes, jewelry, and flowers

   i. Clothes are not for him but for a woman, his lover

   ii. Jewelry often a sign the affair has been going on a while, often given as an anniversary present

   iii. Flowers are given often after an argument or long absence

d. Information on business trips

   i. More out-of-town trips than in previous months or year

   ii. Hotel expenses high for a single guest (sign of room service, such as meals and liquor)

e. Information on second cell phone

   i. Purchased for the lover to make communications between them easier and harder to detect

   ii. Payment for the phone itself, monthly service bill often sent to cheater's office

f. Viagra

   i. Secret purchases made from online pharmacies

g. Individual receipts—can be as valuable as bank and credit card statements

   i. Separate, loose receipts often found in his wallet, briefcase, pants or jacket pockets

    ii. Can be for any expense—restaurants, hotels, gifts, ATM withdrawals

5. Where you should look for statements and receipts
    a. His home office desk drawers and file cabinets (statements)
    b. Briefcase (statements and loose receipts)
    c. Wallet, pants, or jacket (loose receipts, notes with names, phone)
    d. Trash
       i. Incriminating receipts often tossed into the trash
       ii. Most common receipts are from restaurants

By logging the ATM withdrawals, kinds of purchases, and their dates on the following log sheets and then placing the activites and purchases in the matching day of the week on the blank calendar, you could see a pattern displaying the financial costs of the affair, as well as where and how long it's been going on. Not every statement or receipt will supply helpful information, but many could prove to be a gold mine, proving that indeed your husband has been cheating, and you've got the numbers down to the last cent to prove it.

It will likely take some real digging and sleuthing to find the hard numbers such as what you might find in examining his bank and credit card statements. But not all sleuthing requires that you dig through wastebaskets and search his pants pockets for receipts. Now it's time to move on to the hi-tech world of cheating. Certainly the revolution in information technology and communications has given lovers new ways to facilitate conducting their affair. But fortunately for you, technology cuts both ways, as you'll learn in the next chapter.

COMPARISON OF EXPENDITURES LOG

Category: $ Difference:	Est. Amount Spent 1 year ago:	Est. Amount Spent today:
Dining Out $_____	$_____	$_____
Gifts (for you/ family/friends) $_____	$_____	$_____
Clothing $_____	$_____	$_____
Vacations $_____	$_____	$_____
Other "luxury" items $_____	$_____	$_____

UNEXPLAINED/SUSPICIOUS PURCHASES LOG

Date_____ Day of the week _____
Category: Restaurant/Bar_____ Hotel_____ Clothing_____
Jewelry_____ Flowers_____ 2nd Cell Phone _____
Viagra_____ Gift Store_____ Other _____

Amount of purchase $_____
Reason/Excuse _____
(if any) for purchase _____
_____

Date_____ Day of the week _____
Category: Restaurant/Bar_____ Hotel_____ Clothing_____
Jewelry_____ Flowers_____ 2nd Cell Phone _____
Viagra_____ Gift Store_____ Other _____

Amount of purchase $_____
Reason/Excuse _____
(if any) for purchase _____
_____

Date_____ Day of the week _____
Category: Restaurant/Bar_____ Hotel_____ Clothing_____
Jewelry_____ Flowers_____ 2nd Cell Phone _____
Viagra_____ Gift Store_____ Other _____

Amount of purchase $_____
Reason/Excuse _____
(if any) for purchase _____
_____

Date_____ Day of the week _____
Category: Restaurant/Bar_____ Hotel_____ Clothing_____
Jewelry_____ Flowers_____ 2nd Cell Phone _____
Viagra_____ Gift Store_____ Other _____

Amount of purchase $_____
Reason/Excuse _____
(if any) for purchase _____
_____

Date_____ Day of the week _____
Category: Restaurant/Bar_____ Hotel_____ Clothing_____
Jewelry_____ Flowers_____ 2nd Cell Phone _____
Viagra_____ Gift Store_____ Other _____

Amount of purchase $_____
Reason/Excuse _____
(if any) for purchase _____
_____

SUNDAY	MONDAY	TUESDAY	WEDNESDAY	THURSDAY	FRIDAY	SATURDAY

Use this calendar to determine if there is a pattern to the days when the purchases are made. Also, use this calendar to log

CHAPTER 6
The Digital Affair

Today's technologies facilitate infidelity but also provide you with hi-tech warning signs. Benny is one of the best private detectives on our staff. But there's another quality that distinguishes Benny: If it has to do with electronics, Benny is into it. You probably know someone who's like Benny in this way. He's among the first to run to an electronics store to buy the newest, hottest technological innovation, and it's been that way since we first hired him over twenty years ago.

The first cell phone user in our office was Benny; he was likewise the first owner of a DVD player, MP3, and iPod. Benny had TiVo before we even knew anything like that existed, and he was the first to own a flat-screen television. Of course he was taking pictures with a digital camera before anyone else we knew. It's people like Benny—people marketers call "early adopters"—who really introduce the rest of us to the hi-tech devices that in time become a normal, even indispensable, part of our lives.

What's most interesting about Benny's passion for and understanding of advances in consumer electronics is how he's helped our private investigation firmly grasp the importance of technology as it relates to what we do as professionals: catch people who are having affairs. Thanks to Benny and to people like him who are eager to spread the gospel of technology to their friends, family, and coworkers, our society has become quite comfortable with, even blasé about, highly sophisticated new technologies and devices, from laptop computers to digital video games, from PDAs to GPS navigation. In our case, we had the good fortune of having a resident tech guru like Benny at our private investigation firm to show us early in the digital revolution just how certain new technologies would help make cheating easier to commit and to conceal, but also how it would help give *us* new ways to catch the cheaters.

Benny made us aware of how these new advances were changing the way affairs were conducted: cheaters using cell phones instead of pay phones, sending emails instead of letters and notes, making hotel reservations online, turning to adult websites to buy sex toys, and of course searching for lovers from their past and visiting chat rooms and discussion boards to meet new partners. But while cheaters can exploit the newest technologies to help them commit one of the oldest sins, you too can use technology to look for warning signs and catch the cheater in the act.

The Cell Phone and Adultery: A Hi-Tech Tryst

When we first opened our doors, pay phones, which seemed to be located virtually on every street corner back then, were a prime mode of communication for lovers. In countless movies and novels, lovers would plot their rendezvous, reaffirm their love, break up, and reconcile from the pay phone booth. And then the cell phone entered—some would say intruded into—our lives, providing what is undoubtedly one of the most useful tools ever conceived for aiding and abetting adultery. With a single device lovers can communicate by voice, text, or email, and do it at any time from any place. They can furtively send and receive text and email messages on their cell phones even while their spouse is sitting nearby. By offering convenience, privacy, and multiple modes of communication, the now ubiquitous cell phone has become the leading device used by cheaters in planning, executing, and maintaining their affair. No quarters needed.

A Day in the Life of an Affair—with a Cell Phone

While a minority of Americans either by choice or circumstance do not own a cell phone, most of us do have one snuggled in our pocket or purse. And certainly most people having an affair have their cell phone at their beck and call. We know this because in almost every case we handle, the cell phone plays some role, from minor to major. Having worked on thousands of cases where cell phones were involved has proven to us, day after day, how pervasive these devices have become for the cheaters who depend on them.

Small, lightweight, and always at hand, the cell phone has become the adulterer's most-used tool in managing an affair. In the typical day of an affair, lovers might speak a dozen or more times, filling the void between their phone calls with short, often sexually provocative text messages. Often the first cell phone call or text message of the day is made to his lover. If the lovers are apart for any length of time, they use the cell phone to take and send messages and even photos. Rendezvous times and locations are communicated by cell, either by voice, text, or voicemail. In fact, lovers often save their voicemail messages so they can hear each other's voice at the mere push of a button.

During the day the calls and text messages between lovers can dominate all other calls combined. This is especially true on Mondays and Fridays, for on those days lovers either anticipate a reunion (usually on Mondays) or dread their forthcoming separation during a tortuous weekend apart (on Fridays). Lovers will send multiple messages on those days, the messages often crammed closely together, five or ten over just a few minutes, tapering off of course when the lovers reach their home. On the days that lovers plan to meet, which is often the same day or days of the week, cell phone messages, live or voicemail, and text messages fly back and forth with names of restaurants and motels (often coded), stating times and, if needed, locations. The fact is you could track a large portion of the life of an affair by analyzing the call patterns. And that's precisely what we recommend our clients do.

It's His Cell Phone, But It Could Be
Your View into His Affair

The surreptitious, furtive nature of an affair would make you think that lovers would do everything they could to keep the affair a secret from the cheated-on spouse or spouses. And most affairs start off with the lovers' being extremely cautious in covering their philandering tracks—in fact, this hypercaution is usually a hallmark of the beginning weeks or months of an affair. So even if your suspicions of an affair coincide with the affair's actual beginning days, it could prove more challenging to find overt signs during this early period of the affair's life. This does make it more difficult and often not as productive to look for warning signs at the beginning of an affair. But the fact is that most affairs are suspected only after they've been going on for a while—sometimes for many months or even longer. So although there is no general rule of thumb on when affairs become more susceptible to being discovered, the odds are your suspicions will start to gather a while after the affair has commenced.

That's the bad news, and the not-so-bad news (as if there's such a thing as good news regarding your partner's having an affair other than it's over) is that you'll have a better chance of finding the clues that an affair is going on. Lovers who have been seeing each other for months tend to be less cautious and more confident that they won't be caught—after all, they've been seeing each other for a while and as far as they can tell, their relationship remains a secret. When their confidence level reaches that stage, most lovers begin to shed their manically cautious behavior and concern that their every action will reveal a sign of their cheating and betray the affair. This laxity can lead one or both lovers to leave tell-tale indications that range from the slightly suspicious hints (working later than usual) to overt, substantial signs (unaccountable hours) of an affair. And those first sloppy mistakes are often related to how they use—or misuse—their cell phones. That's why we advise our clients to regard their partner's cell phone as a possible treasure trove of information pointing to or even confirming an illicit relationship.

I've Got His Number—How to Check His Cell Phone Without His Knowing

If your spouse senses that you're interested in getting information from his cell phone, we can assure you that he'll do everything possible to erase and remove any even remotely incriminating numbers, saved text messages or phone calls, and photographs. All you'll find will be old messages from you and perhaps a stored photo of your dog. If he notices you eyeing his cell phone as he places it on his nightstand or leaves it on the kitchen counter, there's a good chance he'll suspect that you're doing more than just admiring his choice in cellular devices. So the first lesson is to not display any interest whatsoever in his phone: Don't ask to use it (unless you absolutely need to), don't eye it while it's being charged, don't do a thing that could be construed by him as an indication of your interest in his cell phone. Because if he does sense your interest in his cell phone, he'll go to extraordinary lengths to shield the phone from being successfully explored for information. The goal on your part, then, is to make sure that he harbors no idea that you're dying to get your hands on his phone and the possible information it holds. You can then take advantage of his sense of false confidence.

Creating this false sense of confidence regarding your lack of interest in his cell phone solves one problem in gaining access to possible information his phone holds. But the more daunting task still awaits you: gaining access to his cell phone. There are two components to this effort: The first concerns when it's safe to check out his phone. Obviously you can't do that when he's aware of your handling his phone. We recommend checking his phone when he's indisposed, such as when he's sleeping, occupied in the bathroom (the morning shower is a good time), or doing chores around the house where you can monitor his whereabouts, or other times when he and his cell phone are separated and there's only a slim chance he'll catch you handling the device.

The second challenge in gaining access is in knowing how to operate his cell phone, which could be a different make or model from your own. This means you'll have to learn how to navigate his phone to find the kind of information you're seeking. Obviously when he's in the shower for ten minutes you don't have sufficient time to learn how to operate the alien cell phone in your hands. The reality is that you'll need to know *beforehand* how to operate his phone. Now you might be thinking that learning how to use his cell will be a difficult if not impossible task. Not at all—you learned how to work yours just fine, didn't you? Chances are, his phone's no more confusing than yours, just different. And learning those differences is easier than you may think.

A couple of effective ways accomplish this. Write down the make and model of his cell phone and then visit a cellular store selling that particular phone. Tell the clerk you're interested in that model and have the clerk give you detailed instructions on how to retrieve messages, search for addresses, and view outgoing call records. If the clerk whizzes through each step in a nanosecond, say you need to see the steps again more slowly. Don't leave the store until you have the procedures mastered, writing down each step. The second way to learn how to operate his cell phone is to download the instruction book (if you don't have access at home to his original one). Visit the manufacturer's website and search for the download section, then simply download the instructions for his specific model—most manufacturers have downloads for all models they sell, even discontinued models. In fact, we recommend that you do both: Visit the store for direct instructions from the clerk as well as download the operating manual. A third possibility would be to ask close friends or associates if they have the same phone make and model, and if so, ask to learn how to use the phone.

OK, you've learned how to use his cell phone. Now get to work. Let's say it's Saturday morning and he's started the lawn mower, abandoning his cell phone, which sits on his nightstand. Have the instructions you downloaded close at hand. During the search, don't become so engrossed (or incensed) that you lose track of the time or where your husband is—if the sound of the lawnmower stops, or the water's turned off in the shower, then you should immediately put the cell phone back as you found it. There will be another time. It's more important that you don't get caught than getting to transcribe all the numbers he's called or the text messages he's received in the last couple of days. But assuming that he hasn't erased his latest call and text information and that you safely have the time to do a thorough search, you should be looking for the details of the calls, text messages, and photos to and from his phone. The Cell Phone Calls, Text Messages, and Photos Log on page 129 will help you gather that information.

Besides our most important concern, which is that you must be very careful when gathering the information (if you have any real fear that he might catch you, then don't risk it), there are a few other caveats to consider when determining whether to check his cell phone. First, he may be so paranoid about being caught that he's activated the lock mechanism on his cell phone enabling only someone who knows the password to access the phone's features. If this unlikely but possible situation confronts you, try the passwords you know he uses for other purposes, such as his ATM password. The bad news is that if he has locked his phone and you don't know the password, you're out of luck as far as gaining information from his cell phone—which is all the more reason to hope that you can get hold of the cell phone bills (see next section), which will show all the phone calls and text message calls (though not the actual text messages themselves).

Another precaution he might have taken is to circumvent you completely by purchasing without your knowledge a set of cell phones—one for him, the other for the lover—just to make calls to each other. The only way for you to know about this would be to find the second phone or spot the invoice for the second phone, neither which is probable, but do keep an eye out for either.

The Cell Phone Bill Displays Far More Valuable Information than Just the Amount Due

In a perfect world of accessing information about a possible affair, you'll have the cell phone bills and pertinent information from his cell phone at your disposal. And this does happen. But a more common scenario is having only the cell phone bill to work with, though as you'll see that can be surprisingly helpful. Those long lists of fine print presenting call after call can be a Rosetta stone of information for you, because in those endless columns of phone numbers, durations, and dates lie patterns and signs that can clearly define what's going on—and possibly with whom.

If indeed you are able to locate the cell phone bill, make a photocopy of it and return the original to its exact same location and position—you don't want him to suspect that you've even looked at it, let alone copied it. Now take the following steps to find the most suspicious numbers (some of the steps are tedious, but believe us, they're worth it):

1. Put a line through every number (dialed and received) you're familiar with and that you don't suspect to be involved with any suspicious behavior. That will likely eliminate a large number of calls.

2. Now, focus on the remaining numbers. To make the search manageable, prioritize these numbers by their frequency—the easiest way to do that is to start from the top of the list, taking the first number and counting how many times it appears; then do the same with the second number on the list, and so on through all the numbers. Odds are a few numbers will appear far more regularly than others.

3. Those frequently occurring numbers are the ones to focus on. If any of these numbers shows up on calls made, calls received, text message received, and text message sent, then you've probably isolated the most suspicious number or numbers.

4. Now look at the sequence of the text message calls from the most suspicious number or numbers. Often the text message calls to and from a lover will be grouped, as they serve as a kind of conversation, albeit each remark being a separate call/text message. If you find a number of these packets of calls on a rather consistent basis, it's a serious warning sign of some intense text messaging.

5. Note the days and times of these text messages and of phone calls back and forth from the suspicious number or numbers. Do they occur with some regularity on the same days of the week and perhaps with more frequency on Mondays and Fridays? These are additional signs that the calls are between lovers, not friends or business associates.

Now That You Have the Number, What's Next? Well, It's Your Call (Literally)

You've isolated the most suspicious number or numbers either from the cell phone bill or directly from the cell phone itself or both. The question is: Who *is* this person he's speaking with and text messaging with such regularity and intensity? It's really not possible to find out who the person is, as privacy laws and other statutes would prevent you from discovering whose number it is because most cell phone numbers are unlisted. But there's no law against calling the number, as long as you don't harass the person or commit any other misdemeanor or crime in making the call. Clients have used various approaches, such as calling the number and if someone answers asking to speak with a fictitious person; this way the gender of the person is established as is the fact that the number is still active and used. If our clients hear an outgoing message, we advise them to write down the name if one is given. We discourage making unnecessary and repeated calls to the suspicious number, as this is illegal and usually unproductive. Your goal is to capture the phone number of your spouse's suspected lover, and if possible identify the person he's calling and receiving calls from. Having the phone number is enough to confront him with, once you've gathered additional information, so do not become obsessed with finding out the name and address of the actual person. You'll know soon enough.

You've Got Mail (to Check)

During periods of separation, even for a day or two, a person having an affair often is overwhelmed with the need to feel close to the lover. Today's technologies give cheaters ample ways to connect, even right from home. If your husband has a computer at home, there's a good chance he's using it for more than finishing the spreadsheet for work, visiting eBay, or gathering information on fly fishing in Idaho—he's probably also communicating with his lover by email, chat, and instant messaging. Of course most lovers who communicate with each other using any or all of these means attempt to remove any vestige of the communication. So even if you're able to access his email account, you may be disappointed to find that the surviving email messages are of the regular, innocuous sort relating to work, friends and family, ads, and junk mail—but no gun smoking with a passionate email to or from his lover.

But all is not lost. Numerous devices easily installed on your home computer (or his laptop) will enable you to see—in real time—every email, chat, or instant message he's sending and receiving (see pp. 130-31 for information on this software). Spyware is legal as long as it's installed on a computer that you own; you cannot install it, for example, on his office computer or a computer that is not owned by you unless the owner of the computer consents.

The emails, chats, and instant messaging between lovers will likely reveal an intimacy that transcends the category of warning signs—in fact, the messages could display the indisputable proof that an affair is occurring. Should you find such indicting evidence, we still recommend that you hold off confronting him with the details until you are emotionally and legally prepared to take action and deal with the consequences in ways that keep you in control of the situation.

Tracking the Road to Infidelity

When he says he's meeting the guys for a beer at the sports bar after work to watch the game, and you're suspicious that his plans are far less innocent, we're sure you feel the urge to follow your husband's car to see if he's actually meeting the guys at the bar or his girlfriend at a motel.

Well, now you can sit home and follow his every twist and turn and lie as he drives to a motel or her apartment. The popular GPS devices that you might already own or have seen in action in friends' cars are also available in formats to help suspicious spouses keep track of their husband's precise location without their husband's having a clue. Using the very same technology found on the conventional GPS products sitting on millions of dashboards, these stealth GPS devices are hidden from view under the dashboard or secreted away in some other area of the car. You have a choice of two kinds of clandestine GPS devices as well. One provides a history of your husband's driving activities capturing a precise record of locations and times, which you can download to a computer for review. The other format is also hidden on his car and sends you real-time information of exactly where his car is and how long he's been in a single location. The real-time information is delivered to a Web page accessed only by you. Both these devices can also include a microphone, which picks up conversations in the car that can be recorded or relayed in real time (see p. 132 for details on these GPS devices and where to purchase them).

The Technology Advantage

The last two decades have been a technological boon to those engaged in affairs, providing them with myriad ways to easily and furtively communicate even when in the presence of their spouses, such as sending emails or text messages from home. But these and other technological advances also provide you with powerful tools to catch the cheater, including reading and documenting his emails, text messages, and other forms of digital communications to and from his lover; tracking where he's actually driving; and finding his lover's phone number. And in a small but meaningful percentage of instances, that lover is someone the cheated-on spouse already knows and knows well—because she's a close friend. In the next chapter we show you how to find out if the term "friends and lovers" might apply to your situation.

CELL PHONE CALLS, TEXT MESSAGES, AND PHOTOS LOG

Item   Information to Gather

1. Calls to the phone   Incoming phone number_____
                                        To: name/code of incoming call_____
                                        Time/date_____
                                        Length of call_____

2. Calls from the phone   Phone number called_____
                                        From: name/code/number called_____
                                        Time/date_____
                                        Length of call_____

3. Text messages to the phone   Message_____
                                        From: incoming phone number_____
                                        Name/code of incoming
                                        text messenger_____
                                        Time/date_____

4. Text messages from the phone   Message_____
                                        To: incoming phone number_____
                                        Name/code of incoming text
                                        messenger_____
                                        Time/date_____

5. Photos sent to the phone   Subject of photo_____
                                        From: incoming phone number/name/
                                        code of sender_____
                                        Message, if any_____
                                        Time/date_____

6. Photos sent from the phone   Subject of photo_____
                                        To: phone number and/or name/code of
                                        number called_____
                                        Message, if any_____
                                        Time/date_____

COMPUTER MONITORING SOFTWARE AND DEVICES

Computer monitoring software enables you to automatically and secretly record all activities your spouse performs on your home computer. This includes email, instant messages, files that were accessed, websites visited and other activities. The user will be unaware that the computer is being monitored. The products listed here are among the many computer monitoring software products available. We suggest you review a number of products to see which one is best for your needs and budget (an informational and sales website is listed below each product).

AceSpy Spy Software
www.acespy.net

Email Spy
www.emailspy.com

Invisible Keylogger
www.invisiblekeylogger.net

KEYKatchers
www.youarethespy.com/keykatcher.htm

RemoteSpyware.com
www.remotespyware.com

Spector Pro
eBlaster
www.spectorsoft.com

SpyAgent Computer Monitoring Software
www.spytech-web.com

Spytech Realtime Spy Software
www.spytech-realtime-spy.com

Supreme Spy
www.supremespy.com

Webwatcher Computer Monitoring Software
www.webwatchernow.com

Win-Spy Software Pro
www.win-spy.com

GPS TRACKING PRODUCTS

GPS tracking products are secretly (and usually easily) installed on a vehicle to record (or send in real time) the vehicle's path and location. These products are not inexpensive, running from under $200 to over $500, but they can provide you with an accurate, precise record of where your spouse has driven over a specific time period. The products listed here are among the many GPS tracking products available. We suggest you review a number of products to see which one is best for your needs and budget (an informational and sales website is listed below each product).

MiniTrakPRO
WorldTRAK Real-Time GPS
www.spygear4u.com

PT-200 GPS
Smart Track GPS Tracking System
www.rmtracking.com

Spy Hawk Turbo GPS (real time)
Spy Hawk SuperTrak GPS Worldwide Datalogger
(historical record)
Trackstick II Passive GPS Data Logger (historical record)
www.spyassociates.com

T-Trac XS Internet GPS Car Tracking System
W-Trac GPRS with 15 Second Updates
Livewire FastTrac GPS Tracker
www.brickhousesecurity.com

Various GPS Tracking devices
www.youarethespy.com/gps-tracking.htm

CHAPTER 7
With Friends Like These . . .

"I just *know* he's having an affair, I'm positive of it—but I don't have a clue who he's having it with." We hear some version of that predicament from clients every day. In fact, for many clients the identity of the other woman is at first a mystery, one most clients want us to solve, along with proving for certain that their spouse is cheating. If the suspecting wife has little idea of who the husband is cheating with, we usually pose a question that almost always surprises and often troubles many clients—"Is your husband good friends with a female, including someone the two of you are friends with?" We can reliably predict the response, which usually follows along the lines of a disbelieving, "You're saying he's sleeping with a friend of mine?!" (You may have just heard yourself asking the same question.) Well no. And yes. We ask this provocative question because beyond someone he's met at or through work, friends should be placed near the top of the likely lovers list. And unfortunately this category often leads us to correctly answering the "who" question.

But before we begin to explore the area of affairs with friends, we have a warning signs warning: We emphatically advise that you do *not* regard every female friend the two of you have as a possible candidate who can assume the mantle of the "other woman." In fact, the odds are decidedly against your husband's lover being your close friend, neighbor, or relative. Most cheaters conduct affairs with people their partners don't know or hardly know. So please: Do not be tempted to regard every female the two of you know as your husband's likely lover.

Likewise, do not tell yourself that you can't confide in a female friend about your suspicions that your husband is cheating because you think your confidante could actually be the very same person who is carrying on with your husband. You're likely experiencing a great degree of pain and anger right now, and you don't need to augment this state with unfounded suspicions about your female friends. The reality is, the percentage of cases we work on where the other woman is the wife's close friend or acquaintance is well under one in ten. Because there is only a relatively small chance that you know your husband's lover, it would be unnecessary and ultimately counterproductive for you to focus entirely on your girlfriends as possible candidates. But because there is a chance, and not an insignificant one at that, we do want to discuss how to realistically approach this possibility and how to deal with it. While it's unlikely that the other woman is someone you know, trust, and like (and if no other immediate or solid other clues are yet available), you do need to keep the possibility and your guarded suspicions open.

As you develop a list of likely suspects culled from a roster of female friends, it's important not to allow your suspicions to dominate or control your emotions. In this particular endeavor, as you explore the possibility that your husband might be having an affair with someone you know, and possibly know well, you need to think as clearly and coolly as possible. Revealing and proving a spouse's affair is difficult enough, but the possibility that the other woman is someone you went to the movies with last week has the potential of greatly complicating and exacerbating the profound pain, anger, and humiliation that an affair's revelation can produce. This makes it all the more important for you to eliminate or vastly diminish the odds that not just your husband but a friend of yours has betrayed you. The best way we approach that is to conduct an uncomfortable but necessary examination of possible candidates.

How Friends Become Lovers

Friendships can contribute enormous value and enjoyment to our life, enriching even ordinary experiences, providing comfort, companionship, and support. Most of us take pleasure in nurturing our friendships and are happy, even eager, to expand our cadre of friends. Among the most rewarding aspects of being married is sharing friendships with our spouse. Each partner brings into a new relationship his or her own friends who then become the friends of the mate as well. "My friend" becomes "our friend." And as a couple moves through life together, they acquire friends jointly, be they neighbors or friends of friends, or from friendships formed at work or at church or in the countless ways our friendships are forged. It's of course not surprising that a married couple will share their individually acquired friends. After all, a married couple likely wound up together because they enjoy a preponderance of the same things, share common tastes, have similar preferences, pursue or appreciate the same interests, and by extension enjoy the same kind of people, including each other's friends. So usually a wife will like most of her husband's friends and a husband will get along with most of his wife's friends. You can often tell when a couple has been together for a while, as they refer to "our" friend more frequently than the singular possessive of "my" friend.

While having mutual friends by embracing your partner's friends as your own, by sharing your own friends with him, and by building friendships together, a danger lurks that the compatibility and warm support between good friends of the opposite sex can migrate into something beyond friendship. Opposites do attract, but more often having many interests and likes in common drives a man and woman who are friends to develop a close, warm, and caring relationship. Then time and circumstance can draw the two even closer, and soon each feels there's more attracting them than simple friendship. Also, by its very nature, a close friendship makes us feel more at ease with someone, encourages us to speak more candidly and openly, and to confide our most personal thoughts with little reservation. And opening a window into one's feelings, especially between a man and a woman, can move the intimacy of friendship to another kind of intimacy.

Four Kinds of Friends, the Same Worry

Affairs between friends are as varied as friendships and affairs themselves—from those of short duration to those lasting years, from those that grow stronger to those that simply and slowly fade away. As unique as each affair among friends is, we do see that most affairs between friends fall into one of four categories. There are, of course, other kinds of friendships that turn into affairs, but the vast majority fall roughly into one or more of four categories.

The Best Friend

The affair with the wife's close friend, even her best friend, though she has also become by extension the husband's friend as well.

Susan was my best friend. Now she's become part of one of the worst nightmares I've ever gone through.

I met Susan at my very first Lamaze childbirth class, so that had to have been twelve years ago. We hit it off right from the start, and after our kids were born we remained friends and became closer when Susan and Phil, her husband, split up. David and I would invite Susan and her daughter Meghan over a lot, always on holiday dinners and family celebrations, and we'd go to the town beach with them, stuff like that. I felt good knowing we were helping Susan through a tough time, plus I like Susan—make that liked her—a lot. About maybe six months ago, whenever we'd be together, I began noticing that Susan and David would always end up hanging out together, rinsing and putting the dishes in the dishwasher then staying in the kitchen to talk, or they'd end up walking together if we went to the mall, innocent things like that, but I noticed it. I wasn't jealous, but Susan seemed to be hanging out more with David than with me. Plus, David would be laughing with her a lot but seemed kind of stressed out with me. Then a few weekends ago, David was at soccer with our son, and I went into David's office at home that he set up for the days he telecommutes, looking for some tape. His computer was on, displaying his office email account. I wasn't exactly snooping, but I just thought I should look. I can still feel my face turning red when I saw Susan's emails to him from just that morning alone, each one signed ILU for I Love You! I lost my two best friends that morning.

Patti V.

The New Friend

The affair with a new friend, someone either the husband or his wife has recently met and befriended.

When Latoya moved into the apartment across from us, I thought, "Great!" That was then, this is now.

Now means just six months later, and in that short time our lives have turned upside down. But on that Saturday when Latoya and her sister moved into the apartment right across from us, Tim and I were thrilled. It seemed like everyone around us could have been our grandparents, very nice people, but not the kind to share a beer with. So naturally Tim and me and Toya, which her friends call her, became buddies—her sister was at her boyfriend's 90 percent of the time. Toya was always at our place, or we'd be at her place, kind of like the TV show Friends, *which we all watched together. Must have been a couple of months ago, on a weekend, I asked Tim, who'd been acting kind of quiet, even moody, around me to help with the laundry, and he says he's too busy or something, and we get into a little argument and he snaps at me, "Toya, laundry can wait!" He doesn't even hear himself, but I'm thinking, "Something's wrong here." A little later that morning I tell Tim I'm going shopping and getting a pedicure and will be back in two or three hours. I'm in the car not even ten minutes later when I realize I left my wallet at home so back I go and as I'm walking up the stairs I see Tim and Toya hugging in her doorway and then disappear into her apartment. Since then I've moved out, Tim's begging for me to take him back, and like I said, our world's been turned upside down.*

Bobbie R.

The Old Friend

The affair with an old girlfriend or boyfriend, someone who has resurfaced first as a resurrected friend but then becomes a lover.

I'm not a guy who gets jealous easily. So when Maryanne's ex-boyfriend contacted her, it was fine with me. Not too much is fine now.

I'm more than jealous, I'm furious. But who do I blame? The Internet? Myself for not seeing what was happening? Maryanne, yes, sure. And more than anyone, Doug, her ex. But before all the blame and all the hurt there was the short, innocent-looking message posted on one of Maryanne's social networking sites she belongs to, this one for teachers—Maryanne's a teaching administrator. "Are you Maryanne so-and-so who lived in San Diego ten years ago," and long story short, her ex, Doug, whom she lived with before we met now lives here in Houston with his new wife. We're all adults, so we arrange dinner, and it's all fine—like I said, I'm not the jealous type, and Maryanne and Doug were an item years and years ago. And to tell you the truth I liked both Doug and Allie. So we'd see them every so often, but I noticed that after each dinner or movie or whatever, Maryanne would make some cutting comment about Allie, like "Can you believe the outfit she wore," or "What a stupid answer" to some question I asked Allie, never a compliment, always a little dig. Looking back I can see this was when Maryanne started working late, usually on Mondays or Wednesdays and sometimes both. Plus, she started going to the office on Saturdays, saying that with so many new teachers there was a lot more work. With all the work she was always too tired for sex, or at least that's what she told me. But I was still living in the dark, sensing something's wrong but not putting it all together. Then comes the call to me from Allie who wants to know what I know about Doug and Maryanne's seeing each other. It gets worse. Allie had hired a private investigator and wants to show me photos of them kissing in a parking lot and other photos of Maryanne and Doug entering a motel room. Talk about a blast from the past.

Martin G.

The Phantom Friend

The affair with a phantom friend, so named because he speaks of this new friend with growing frequency; she's likely someone he works with but has become a confidant, perhaps a lunch mate or drinking buddy after work.

Work and work—those were Randall's two passions. Now it looks like he has gotten himself a third.

And it's called Melissa. Melissa, as in the woman who was his lover, mistress, concubine, whatever, for at least six months or more—I still can't get the story straight from him other than he says it's over, over, over. And now that I know, I can look back and see that the signs were pretty much there from the beginning. Like when Randall started mentioning the great new public relations firm and its hotshot account executive that Randall's company hired. Because he's always talking about work it sometimes goes in one ear for me and out the other, but I remember this one because he's usually not that overtly complimentary about people he works with. And it seemed like a few times a week she'd end up in his stories about work, Melissa suggested this or did that, all of which according to Randall, was terrific, smart, great. I knew they'd have lunch together, business lunches, Randall wouldn't hide that, and drinks too, as she worked for the public relations firm they use. So I didn't think much of this, after all, he'd mention it to me, not like his friendship with her was a big secret, and let's be honest here, Randall's a fifty-five-year-old corporate executive, and this Melissa, from what I could tell, was a late twenties-something lower-level PR person, so what's to get suspicious about? Even when Randall and I were at a restaurant, and he says out of nowhere that waitress over there looks a lot like Melissa, same hair and eyes—this from someone who normally wouldn't notice if our waiter was taking our order standing in a tutu— I'm really not suspicious. Then with the annual industry conference coming up over in Chicago, Randall says he's going to leave two days early for it this year and stay an extra day. "Melissa and her team and I need to make presentations to the press," he says; still sounds like nothing to worry about. But when he comes home from the conference, he announces that he wants a trial separation. Three months later, though it feels like three decades, we're trying to work it out, which is going to be the biggest job he's ever had.

Lauren A.

The Tip-Offs

What clues should you look for when suspecting that he's having a "friend affair," which is how we refer to this particular category of affairs? Let's review some of the most common indications.

It's (Not) All in a Name

One of the most common (and least subtle) clues that he's having an affair with someone you know is when he mentions her name more frequently than usual. Friends are often topics of conversation between couples, as we're all amateur gossip columnists of sorts, finding pleasure in discussing other people's lives; friends also serve as points of reference in a conversation, such as, "Their son reminds me of Jim and Deb's oldest, the math whiz." So while the names of friends weave their way throughout our daily lives, when a name—a female friend's name—seems to your ear to be mentioned more than it used to be, make a note of this increase.

Also note the context in which her name is brought up, giving special attention to the relevance or need to use her name. Why would he find it necessary to mention that your friend Regina likes Tom Hanks when the two of you are in the car heading to a new Tom Hanks movie? Innocent and isolated as these mentions of a friend may appear, the accumulation of many otherwise inconsequential statements that include a female friend's name can serve as a clue that he's more than friends with her. Perhaps at this stage he's merely infatuated with her; but it could likely be more than that. Or maybe it's only a coincidence that her name has come up with far more regularity than it has in the past. This clue then certainly is neither conclusive proof nor even a leading indicator of betrayal. But it can play a supporting role in a group of more substantial clues showing a growing and probably unhealthy relationship beyond friendship.

Criticizing a Friend's Spouse

Besides his bringing up her name with what might be considered inordinate frequency (and often unnecessarily), also take notice if he seems critical of her husband or partner, especially if he hasn't spoken negatively about her spouse before. Attacking or making derogatory statements and slights about your friend's husband or partner serves as a kind of defense of your husband's own infidelity, in a way sanctioning his inappropriate behavior.

Lovers are almost always jealous of and angry with the spouse of their lover; they view the spouse as an encumbrance to their own relationship and as the other person their lover is sleeping with. As with the clue of bringing up her name with unusual consistency, this clue—making critical, disparaging remarks about your friend's spouse—is not conclusive proof, even when combined with his mentioning her name again and again. But together, these two clues should focus your attention on a friend as a person of special interest.

She's My Friend, Too You, Know

A married couple shares many things, some would say everything, and that includes friends. But when does sharing a friend of the opposite sex shift from something to accept, encourage, and appreciate into something to worry about? Say you and your husband are very friendly with a couple whom you see a few times a month, go out to dinner with regularly, catch a movie with on occasion, maybe go camping with, and watch each other's houses when the family is away. But recently you're noticing that your husband and the wife of the other couple often end up together, chatting in the kitchen, working the barbecue grill, arranging a friendly lunch during the week. Is this a natural part of being friends, or is it something to worry about or even become a tad jealous over?

Jealousy is not an admirable emotion, because it brings out our basest instincts and characterizes us as acting in trivial, self-absorbed, childish ways. But when you suspect that your husband is having an affair—and possibly one with someone you know—it's hard to escape the feelings of jealousy and possessiveness or to keep them in check. In this case you might be right to feel jealous, but now is not the time to confront him with questions about the apparently growing closeness with your female friend.

If your partner is a naturally friendly person, gregarious even, and enjoys being with others, then factor in those traits when gauging if his warmth toward a woman friend warrants serious concern. We're not saying that you should dismiss your concern because your husband is "a people person," but do consider that his friendliness with a female friend of yours might not mean that she's the other woman. That said, his natural friendliness might be disguising his deeper feelings for her. On the other end of the personality spectrum lies the husband who rarely exhibits interest in being close with the female side of a couple you know but now is unabashedly friends with her. If this latter description fits your husband, then the warning signs flag should be raised.

And even if your husband's personality falls somewhere in between the two extremes—neither overtly outgoing, who seems to like just about everyone he meets, nor reclusive with only a couple of close buddies—you should be aware of his developing a closer than normal (for him) friendship with a woman friend. The friendship might be totally innocent and healthy for all concerned, but if you're already suspicious of his having an affair then it makes perfectly good sense to keep your eye on his congenial ways with the female half of your couple friends. Or any female friend of his for that matter.

Who Did You Just Call Me?

Now let's move upward on the list of signs to watch for in determining if your husband might be having an affair with a woman friend you know, starting with a telling, and more than embarrassing, slip of the tongue. Our mind works in ways that perhaps make it seem at times like an uncontrollable child, doing exactly the opposite of what we want. This is especially obvious when we say a word or phrase that we're otherwise careful to keep from uttering, which often occurs in times of stress. One of our favorite stories in this regard was told by Anne Morrow Lindbergh about her mother. When Anne was a small child, the fabulously wealthy J. P. Morgan was invited for a visit. "Now, Anne," her mother instructed, "you must not say one word about Mr. Morgan's nose," referring to the multimillionaire's famously huge and bulbous nose. Anne was quiet when Morgan arrived, but upon pouring a cup of tea for him and dipping a spoon into the sugar bowl, her mother politely asked, "Will you have one or two lumps in your nose?"

We've all made stupendously embarrassing remarks, usually at moments of stress or fatigue. And conducting an affair can add great emotional strain and anxiety to one's life. Many clients have said that their husbands call them by the wrong name and often without the husband even noticing it. But *you* certainly should notice it—especially if the wrong name he calls you is also the name of a good friend of yours. If this happens, act like you didn't hear his faux pas or that you weren't sure what he said. Also note the context in which he's calling you by the wrong name. For example, was he noticeably nervous? Or even amorous (as the wrong name pops up in the bedroom too)? And did this occur on a weekend or some other time when the lovers would be away from each other and her name would be on his mind? Also, be prepared: Chances are the first time he calls you by her name might not be the last. In each occurrence, rather than correcting him, pretend you weren't paying attention, but note the day and the context of the miscall.

On the Payroll

Another serious sign of trouble arises when a husband, often with little notice to or consultation with his wife, hires the wife's friend to work for him or strongly recommends the friend for a position where he works. If you already have suspicions about the two of them, you should be very concerned about this employment situation. Now it certainly isn't uncommon for friends to hire friends or to be instrumental in helping a friend land a job in the same place of employment. Friends do end up working together, especially if one of them is looking for work and the other has a position or knows of a position that's open—after all, what are friends for? But if your husband comes home one evening announcing that he's just hired one of your friends as his associate marketing director, you should feel right in not wanting to necessarily celebrate her good fortune in employment. This especially rings true if the friend is, in your estimation, underqualified or even totally unfit for the job or project. If the two of them are lovers, then the job was offered to her as a way for them to spend more time together, even if it's a part-time job or project.

If your husband's explanation for hiring or recommending your friend for a job in the same company seems forced, unrealistic, or contrived, your fears should not only increase but are more likely to be confirmed. However, at this stage you should appear to be noncommittal, disinterested, or if you can manage the act, even delighted at your husband's largesse at hiring or helping out a good friend. But in reality, you should be searching for any and all other relevant signs that your husband is having an affair—because now you might have a good idea of who he's having it with.

He Receives More Email from Her than from Anyone Else (Including You)

Most working adults who have Internet access and email accounts likely receive many messages daily, including numerous personal emails. For many of us, personal emails eclipse ones we send and receive for business purposes. So checking your spouse's email—without his knowing it—has the potential of giving you volumes of insight about who he's communicating with and what he's saying or reading. Even if you do have brief access to his email account on his home computer, the risk of getting caught plying through his messages makes the exercise potentially dangerous. We discussed various products and services that allow you to remotely capture his emails found on his home computer without his knowledge, or to have emails he's deleted retrieved from his trash (see pp. 130–31). But short of using sophisticated tools such as these, it's still possible to glance at his email page to see from whom he's receiving (and to whom he's sending) numerous emails. Of course you can't say, "Honey, can I take a peek at your email inbox for a few minutes?" But you can send him an email with an attachment—say, a photo—and tell him that you want to see how it looks after you email it, which is an innocent-sounding request. As he pulls up his email, try to quickly scan all the others on the page, looking for familiar email addresses from friends of yours. Lovers often send more emails over the weekend or when they're apart, so try this tactic on a Saturday or Sunday afternoon. And if you do see a familiar address, one from a female friend of yours, your warning signs flag should begin billowing.

What a Coincidence!

Should two or more of the above signs point to the fact that your husband is cheating with someone you know, then you have reason to start proving the hypothesis conclusively. Begin by seeing if both your husband and your friend are unavailable at the same time on a consistent basis—not an easy exercise at all but one you should try to conduct, as it could help to expose the truth one way or another. If your husband and the friend disappear for a few hours at the same time over a period of days or weeks, these dual and identical absences are hardly coincidences. Write the days and the times of these "coincidences" in the blank calendar on page 157 to see if there is a pattern.

If you have become suspicious because your husband works late more than usual, the next time he calls to say he'll be working into the evening or is having dinner with a client, call the home of the friend you suspect he's having the affair with. And be sure to have a legitimate excuse to be calling her in case she (or her possibly duped spouse) picks up the phone. Don't call her cell phone, as it will likely display your number which could tip her off that you're suspicious, as there'd be no reason to be calling her cell if she should be home. And even if she's with your husband she could still answer her cell and signal him to remain quiet while she talks to you. If she's not at home on three or more incidences that coincide with your husband's working late or running extra-long errands on weekends, then you should suspect that there's more going on here than a stream of coincidences. To establish if there's a pattern to these incidences, use the blank calendar on p. 157 to write in the evenings when he's working late and the friend you suspect he's cheating with is not at home.

If they work together (after his generously getting her a job), then they may conduct their affair during lunch or right after work. At those times, call her cell phone, though not from your home or cell phone, which can identify you—use a pay phone, and if she answers, simply hang up so she thinks it's a wrong number or incomplete call. It's more likely, if they are having an affair, that you'll get her cell phone's voicemail. Then, a few minutes later, call your husband's cell phone, using your own cell or landline phone, so he knows it's you calling. Have a good reason to be calling him, such as stopping by the grocery to get milk; odds are he won't answer. Do this a few weeks running but only on days that you suspect they're seeing each other, which, as we've said, is often the day before or the day after the weekend separation. Keep a log of the times you suspect they might be spending time together, as well as the times you called each of them, and note the results of each call. And if you see a pattern develop, where both your husband and your friend are not at their job or home at the same time, incident after incident, you're looking at a very potent Warning Sign.

On the other hand, we've had many cases where the suspecting wife was certain the husband was having an affair with a close friend of hers only to find out from our surveillance that the woman her husband was cheating with was a total stranger to her. Or a few times the other woman turned out to be a *different* friend from the one the wife suspected. These cases demonstrate that in suspecting that a good friend or someone you know well is having an affair with your husband, you do need to tread as carefully as possible. Don't rush to conclusions, and as we said, don't place every woman friend you have on the most-wanted list.

To Tell or Not to Tell

In most cases when the husband is having an affair with a friend of his wife's, that friend also has a husband or partner the cheating husband and his wife are likely to be friends with. Using the tools we discussed in this and other chapters, if you discover that the wife of a good friend is having an affair with your husband, should you inform that husband? And if so, when?

The answer is not always simple. There's little doubt that your anger, even rage, could lead you to contact the husband of the wife your husband has cheated with, giving him the details of betrayal you both have suffered. But it's vital to recognize that your greatest challenge at that point will be to deal with your own marriage, not to also become involved with the struggles that have befallen another's no matter how intricately linked the marriages have become. When your husband's infidelity is exposed to him and to his lover, the entire dynamic of your marriage will shift. Taking on the added burdens in dealing with two marriages in disarray could be overwhelming and lead not to healing and moving on but to added chaos and endless recriminations that only deepen and prolong the pain. In our experience, once one side of the affair is revealed, all is exposed to all concerned. Her husband will find out perhaps only hours after you confront your husband, either by the guilty wife or by mutual friends you share the news with. And it's likely the cheating wife has left her own legacy of clues; nevertheless, once an affair is exposed, those close to the participants know the truth or at the very least that something is drastically wrong and has to be addressed.

Your needs demand that you face and deal with your own pain, your own decisions, your own life. We urge you to consider the enormity and complexity of those duties and how they can be compromised if you also become involved with the travails the other woman has inflicted on her own marriage.

Turning to Dr. Gunzburg: An Avalanche of Questions

Any affair causes an earthquake, its shockwaves ripping deep inside us. As Bobbie R. put it in her story on pp. 137–38, your world can feel like it's been turned upside down. And when the affair was with a friend or close associate, the shock can be of a greater magnitude. But even if you don't know the other person or didn't know her well, the shock is huge, and the ramifications can be massive. Understanding how most people react to the news can help you better handle the trauma and begin to work on healing yourself and, if you can, your relationship.

The first thing to recognize is that *you are not alone.* Every day thousands of couples face the reality that an affair has been going on. Many more times that number are struggling with the aftermath of an affair, whether it's trying to rebuild their marriage or deciding what to do next. But when the affair is first revealed, all couples share very similar reactions; the most common reaction is posing a set of questions that are so consistently alike from couple to couple and person to person, it seems as if all couples were living the same trauma. And in certain respects they were. These more or less universal questions, which I cover here, can help you to frame your situation and guide you in how to successfully begin to navigate through the healing and recovery process. They also prove to you that you are not at all alone in this, as lonely as you might feel at this moment.

How Could This Happen to Us?

There are really two parts to this question. The first, of course, is the utter sense of disbelief that anything like this could have happened. This disbelief can be compounded when the other person turns out to be a friend. Even if she isn't anyone you know, or know well, the very idea that an affair could occur causes a sense of almost perverse wonderment: How on earth did something like this happen to people like us? But the second component to the question revolves around the deeper question: How could things have gotten to the point where this was the result? In short, how could this even happen? It's this part of the question that each couple needs to grapple with in order to begin the healing process. At this point in time, however, with the wound still so fresh, you need to pay attention to what you're feeling and dealing with at this very moment.

How Long Has This Thing Been Going on between You Two?

It's bad enough to know that your spouse has betrayed you, but if that betrayal was conducted with someone you know, you can feel even more like a fool. But the fact is, no matter with whom he's had the affair—someone you've known for years or someone you've never met and likely will never meet—you probably feel as if you were blind to it all and easily and totally duped. In the case of the affair happening with a friend, you may feel as if you allowed your friendship to be taken advantage of too, making you feel even more like a fool or dunce.

But let's get something straight right from the start. There is no reason to be harsh on yourself for being the victim of lies and deceptions. It's not a sign of some profound character flaw or intellectual deficiency that your partner lied to you. You were not acting stupidly, you were not a dunderhead, you were not deficient at all. But you *were* deceived. The fact that you didn't see it coming or you didn't have the benefit of Tony's and Dawn's professional advice about warning signs in time, doesn't label you as naïve or gullible. It does mean you were cheated on, but that is your partner's fault, not yours. This also holds true if the lover had been a friend of yours—that fact shouldn't make you feel incompetent or dimwitted, only sad and very, very angry.

If the affair hasn't been exposed yet and you're still just suspicious, the tools that Tony and Dawn are equipping you with to recognize the warning signs will make you feel that in the end you weren't mistaken in your having suspicions; as it might likely happen, you could be the one who finds out what was going on. That said, you will still have to grapple with the reality of the issue itself.

And Just How Many People Know about This?

It's not uncommon for others—friends, family, or business associates—to know about the affair before you do. This is especially true if the affair is with someone you know such as a good friend, coworker, or unfortunately a family member. And you might feel an even heightened sense of betrayal from all those individuals who chose not to share the information with you. The best way—I feel, the only way—to handle that is to understand that what's happened is between you and your husband and no one else, not even the lover, friend of yours or not.

Do others owe it to you to provide the facts, the whole truth? That's a separate question and an enormously complex one that will only be answered over time, hopefully with the benefit of constructive conversations with these up-to-now silent witnesses. But that's then—right now the affair and its aftermath are strictly between you and your partner. And you need to deal with that and how you move forward.

How Can I Ever Again Have Trust in My Partner?

Who could blame you for asking that? Here's the one person you have given your personal trust, your love, your attention, and your future to—and it's all been betrayed. No wonder you might feel right now that you could never, ever trust him again. And if the affair was with a friend of yours, it might seem all but impossible that you could ever trust someone who's done this to you and your family.

But you can trust again, unlikely as that might sound—but only if he commits himself to regaining your trust. This means being totally honest, open, and transparent, as well as proving to you in other ways that once again he deserves and has earned your sacred trust. All of this takes commitment, perseverance, and openness from both of you. But yes, improbable as it might seem right now, you can trust your partner again.

Is This the Only One, or Have There Been Others?

The short answer, and probably the safer one, is who knows? It's far harder to prove that a previous affair or affairs occurred in years past, even with all the tools that are provided in this book. Maybe with a large investment of money and resources you could prove that there have been earlier affairs but probably not. That said, all the research and statistics in the area do show that when people cheat one time, there's a high probability that they'll do it again. And if this earlier infidelity or infidelities were successful—no one was caught and the partners for the most part were satisfied with the experience—it's even more likely that it will reoccur. But each affair is unique, as is each couple's recovery. And recovery and the future is where to look now, not fixating on possible earlier affairs. Your bigger concern should be if he is changing his own character so he becomes the person who would never have an affair (in the future) and the person who manages his own behavior so he won't take even a first step that could risk leading to an affair.

Am I Overreacting Here?

The short answer is a resounding no. However, I am making the assumption that you are not causing physical harm to your spouse and that you are not involved in extreme vengeance such as having an affair yourself, causing your family to go into financial ruin, announcing the affair in a public gathering where you are known, or some other extreme behavior. If you didn't feel your partner's having an affair was a big deal or not that worrying or even understandable, you'd be reacting in a most abnormal way. In fact, feeling hurt and being almost overwhelmed by negative feelings are two of the most common ways that someone acts after discovering infidelity.

Being married or involved in a monogamous relationship means you trust your partner to be faithful—it's a cornerstone of any intimate relationship. It's important to note that while fidelity helps to make a relationship stable and secure, it is not the entire foundation of that stability and security. Still, when trust is fractured by infidelity, you feel far less secure, loved, and safe. Reacting to this by having negative thoughts—some of them quite intense and disturbing—is normal.

Why Do I Feel like a Doormat?

If you're asking this question, you probably think you're being foolish. When people ask this, what they're really asking is whether they're being foolish in even thinking about trying to rebuild their marriage. Understand that most people do want to rebuild their marriage, and that includes the person who has been hurt as well as the person who's caused all the pain. If the lover was a close friend of the cheated-on lover as we saw in some of the stories in this chapter, the healing process is more complicated and difficult, especially at the beginning. However, that should not deter a couple from wanting to give their marriage and their lives a second chance, as improbable as that might sound right now.

The most important point is that there's no doormat issue at all when you're thinking about keeping the door open to rebuilding your marriage.

Is This Relationship Doomed?

No, not if you both want it to work. And relationships in far worse shape than yours have survived and thrived. An affair doesn't doom a relationship—how the couple responds to the affair is what determines if any relationship can survive, heal, and grow. It takes hard work and a total commitment to success to rebuild the trust and rejuvenate a marriage. I don't know your own situation, but I've very likely helped many couples whose marriage was in very similar straights as your own marriage is, or might be, right now. They made it. So can you, as hard as that might be to believe right now.

The Friend Affair

One of the first questions a person who's been cheated on asks is, "Who's the other person?" When the answer turns out to be someone she knows, like a close friend, the pain of the affair can be *multiplied,* for now there's been a double deceit. Though it's highly unlikely that the affair you suspect or will have to contend with is with a friend of yours, you still need to be prepared for the possibility. There are four basic kinds of affairs with friends:

1. The affair with the wife's close friend who's become the husband's friend as well
2. The affair with a new friend, whom one of you has recently befriended
3. The affair with an old girlfriend or boyfriend who has recently resurfaced
4. The affair with a phantom friend he works with but who has become a confidant

The most important clues from your spouse to look for in a friend affair are

- Mentioning her name with growing frequency, especially in ways and at times that lead you to believe that he's thinking about her
- Being hypercritical of your friend's spouse, often unfairly or in unwarranted ways
- Spending more time with the friend, even if it's in front of you in very open and social settings
- Accidentally—and often unaware that he's doing it —calling you or someone in your family by your friend's name
- Hiring, being influential, or helpful in securing your friend a job in the same place where he works

- Receiving email from her and perhaps trying to hide the fact from you
- Being unreachable at the same times that your friend is likewise unavailable

When a husband has an affair with one of his wife's friends it adds the complicated question of whether to notify the husband of the other woman. We suggest that our clients deal with their own concerns first. Dr. Gunzburg also feels that an affair is the business of the husband and the wife and no one else, at least when it's first exposed and the work of healing has to begin.

Most of us feel that hardly anything could be worse than discovering the affair has been with a close friend. But two categories of warning signs eclipse even the knowledge that a friend has played a role—one is contracting a sexually transmitted disease, and the other is being abused. While neither one is a dominate warning sign, both are regularly cited by our clients and infidelity experts. And when it comes to how you find out if an affair is going on, you need to know about every possible clue. We explore each in the next chapter.

SUNDAY	MONDAY	TUESDAY	WEDNESDAY	THURSDAY	FRIDAY	SATURDAY

Use this calendar to determine if there is a pattern to when both parties are not at home.

CHAPTER 8

From the Obvious to the Dangerous—Final Clues

The arsenal of clues and signals you've acquired so far in *Warning Signs* has armed you with insights and skills that enable you to recognize—and very likely expose—an ongoing affair. Thanks to all the myriad investigative techniques, tips, and guidance we've provided—from studying his credit card receipts for meals and gifts that bear suspicious activities to reading his body language to interpret the vocabulary of his unabashed lies; from perceiving the importance of seemingly innocuous and trivial changes in his behavior, dress, and routines to tracking down his whereabouts when he's not where he's supposed to be; and more—you've become a versed, knowledgeable, and savvy sleuth.

But we're not yet done. The remaining final signs are the last, not because they are the least important of all the signs nor because we regard them as the most vital and critical ones—the fact is, the most important warning signs are the ones that work for *you,* the ones that do the most effective job of helping you get at the truth. We complete our tally of signs with these two groups because neither fits neatly into the other categories of signs, yet both certainly bear mentioning in a book dedicated to helping you recognize and respond to the warning signs of a cheating spouse. One group represents the most obvious of clues, while the other identifies the most sinister and dangerous of signs. The former group comprises clues that are blatant, unambiguous signs of infidelity—so much so, you certainly don't need matrimonial private investigators like us to suggest that you recognize them as indicators of cheating. But we present them here because no collection of signs of adultery would be complete without them. And the same holds true for the other category, signs that go beyond indicating an affair is going on, as they also can impose serious physical or mental harm to you and possibly to your family—and we hope it's highly unlikely that you'd be exposed to such signs. We'll review both categories now, starting, appropriately, with the obvious.

"Cincher" Clues

It's become a worn cliché of sorts, though it remains an obvious and serious sign of cheating: While routinely doing her family's laundry, a wife discovers the soft smudge of another woman's lipstick or makeup staining her husband's white shirt collar. Hackneyed as the clue is, we can assure you that it happens and more frequently than you'd think. That said, our clients aren't reporting the makeup-on-the-collar clue as often as they did perhaps ten or twelve years ago, likely because of the decline in sales of men's white dress shirts over the past decade or so. Fewer and fewer men are donning neckties these days, opting instead for sports shirts of various hues, white often not being one of them. It's simply not as easy as it used to be to spot that tell-tale smear of Revlon Super Lustrous Lipstick (not in your shade). So a single cultural change—more casual and colorful men's apparel at work—has diminished the ranking of one of the classic, obvious warning signs that a husband is cheating. We call these undeniable and indisputable signs "cinchers," as they tell us that it's for sure—a cinch—that an affair is likely going on. Lipstick on the collar still ranks as a cincher, but fashion trends have certainly ratcheted down its usefulness.

L'air du Deceit

Another classic cincher endures and is as prevalent as in years past. An alien perfume (that is, a brand not sitting on *your* dresser or vanity tray) wafting from a husband's shirt or his body is an irrefutable sign that he's been very close to another woman. A one-time episode of his shirt holding the lingering scent of perfume should raise a warning-sign flag, but it's certainly less than conclusive proof. But a second occurrence or multiple instances of his coming home smelling more like L'air du Temps than Calvin Klein Man means he's very likely becoming intimate with someone else. In the last eight or nine years, another cincher has made its appearance, supplying suspecting wives with evidence that their husbands are having sex outside of marriage. That cincher is Viagra.

His Secret Stash of Viagra Indicates a Different Kind of Dysfunction

Ever since Viagra was introduced in the late 1990s, tens of millions of prescriptions have been written to help men suffering from an authentic medical condition, penile dysfunction. But almost immediately after its appearance, Viagra took on the aura of a magical enhancer of a man's sexual performance. In fact, the drug does not increase the sexual prowess of most men, though it is highly effective in doing what it's prescribed to address: aiding men suffering from penile dysfunction. But through word of mouth, much of it misinformed, Viagra's taken on the image of a transformative sexual elixir, one that turns men into superpotent sexual partners. Small wonder then that many of our clients report that their husbands began getting prescriptions for Viagra around the same time that other signs indicated that another woman might be benefiting from Pfizer's wonder drug. And other clients were even more suspicious that an affair was going on because they were not supposed to even know that their husbands were taking the medication. Instead, these women just happened to come upon their husbands' private, hidden stash or found a prescription in their partner's papers. A cincher, to be sure.

Of course, millions of men do suffer from penile dysfunction, and Viagra is a wonderful medication for that unfortunate condition. But because of the reputation Viagra has gained as an enhancer of sexual performance, real or imagined, your husband's keeping a secret stash of it is a sign that he wants to be a stellar performer in bed. And that bed isn't the one he shares with you.

Finding Items Not Meant for Your Eyes—or Your Bedroom

Some cheaters, as we've noted, are hypercautious, obsessed with covering their tracks, doing anything and everything they can to conceal the affair they're conducting. But in our experience the majority of cheating spouses might think they're successful in hiding their adultery but inevitably leave unambiguous, obvious, and damning clues—the cinchers—that reveal the depth of their guilt. Among the most incriminating physical evidence indicating that a partner is having sex outside marriage are items the suspecting wife uncovers inside her husband's briefcase or home office desk, in his gym bag, toolkit, dopp kit, or any secure place that the cheater believes his wife has no interest in or never peruses. The list of these items our clients have unearthed reads like a catalog from an Internet sex shop: condoms (often with exotic attributes), lubricants, sex toys of all manner and inclination, pornographic material, sexy undergarments—like we said, a veritable catalog of sexual enhancement products.

In fact, clients often tell us they have to visit the website of companies selling sexual aid products to ascertain the purpose of some of the devices and items; in finding out, these women become even more repulsed by their husband's double life. And the Internet is likely where their husbands bought the products in the first place, as the Web has made it far easier to purchase sexual products. Many men no longer have to patronize sex shops often located in the seedier parts of town or worry about being seen by friends or associates walking out of Shirley's Sexy Treasure Trove. Now they can shop online and have the products discreetly delivered to their office. So no one knows they've bought sexual products, other than their lover—and their wives who find condoms in the bottom of the husband's briefcase.

Should you come upon such a collection of items, or even a single hidden condom (especially if he doesn't use condoms with you), do not move them or give any sign that you've discovered such indicting proof of his cheating on you. Rather, keep as cool as you can, record the date and the details, such as what the items are and where you uncovered them. Should the stash contain condoms, count how many are there, without moving or shifting any other items; return to the site, if possible, every few days to see if the number of condoms has changed. In this way, you can approximate how often he's having sex with his partner. If at all possible, take a photo of the sexual loot, but be sure not to keep the photo or the digital file of it any place where your spouse could find it. By keeping the stash as undisturbed as possible, you lower the chances of his suspecting that you even know they're there. At the appropriate time, you'll use this evidence to confront him, to thwart him from denying that he's cheated or from saying your suspicions are just a figment of your overactive imagination. Some figment, some imagination.

Extreme Signs: Warning Signs That Are Dangerous to Your Health and Safety

It's hurtful enough to find the obvious cinchers—the hard, tangible evidence such as lipstick smears or the scent of another woman's perfume on your husband's clothes or a package of condoms tucked away in his briefcase. But a small but meaningful percentage of our clients are exposed to far more painful evidence that their husband is having an affair, evidence that affects their emotional health, their physical well-being, and even their lives. Though it's extraordinarily unpleasant to imagine your spouse endangering you in such an extreme way, for your own safety and perhaps the safety of your children, you need to be made aware of the following risky and dangerous signs.

Bringing the Affair Home—through Sexually Transmitted Diseases (STDs)

We are all too familiar with the pain our clients suffer as they come to the recognition that their spouse is most likely, or definitely, in the midst of an affair. The emotional pain can be excruciating, though you *will* survive. For some of our clients, however, the hurt caused by their husband's sabotaging the mutual trust that all relationships need to survive is compounded when they become infected with an STD their husband has contracted from his lover. While some psychologists and medical ethicists argue that adultery itself is a sign of some unfulfilled emotional need and should therefore be categorized as a condition to be treated, there's no argument about the real and present dangers that any one of the host of STDs can inflict upon a woman.

Should you suffer from symptoms that lead you to suspect that you've been infected with an STD we discuss in this section, you must place the need to attend to the STD ahead of virtually any other need, including lashing out at your husband for adding illness to the insult of infidelity. An STD can produce very serious consequences, so it is vital that you receive medical attention if you have any reason to believe that you've been infected. Also, immediately cease from having further sexual relations of any kind with your spouse; if medical professionals do confirm that you have contracted an STD, you must notify your husband who is likely unaware that he is carrying and infected with the disease.

Each of the STDs addressed here can be contracted solely through sex (except for human immunodeficiency virus [HIV], which can be contracted through contaminated blood), be it vaginal, oral, or anal. (In most cases, an infected pregnant mother can pass the disease along to the baby during vaginal delivery.) You cannot become infected through contact with a toilet seat or airborne bacteria. It takes sex, which means if you do become infected with an STD and the only person you're having sex with is your husband, then he is the source of your disease. And the only way he could have infected you is by sleeping with another person who has the STD. There are exceptions to this. For example, he may have acquired the STD years earlier, even before the two of you were intimate, and the disease has remained dormant until now. But in the majority of cases, an STD is acquired and spread in rapid order, which means if you begin to display active symptoms, and your husband has been your sole sexual partner, then your marriage has been contaminated not just with the loss of trust but by the introduction of an STD.

Additionally, even if you are not displaying any signs of having been infected by an STD, but you know your husband is sleeping with another person, you should ask your doctor if a test for an STD is advisable. Considering that some STDs do not display symptoms, or they display very mild ones that are easy to overlook, many health care professionals feel the prudent and wise course is to take STD tests if a spouse has sex with another person.

What You Need to Know about Some Diseases You Really Don't Want to Know About

Should you have symptoms of any one or more of the STDs discussed here, immediately stop having any form of sex with your husband and seek the help of medical professionals. If the medical professionals confirm that you have contracted an STD, follow their treatment programs and tell your spouse you are infected. Even if he denies that he could possibly be the one who gave it to you, it is important that he knows and can attend to getting treatment for himself. He should, of course, immediately inform his lover, which is his responsibility.

Chlamydia

This is the leading bacterial STD, the one that's reported more frequently than any other. Common as it is, it can be overlooked by many of the people infected by it, as its symptoms can be very mild or not noticeable at all. If your husband has indeed been having an affair, and you've had sex with him during that period, ask your doctor or health professional if an STD test, including one for chlamydia, should be conducted as a precaution. Chlamydia, like all STDs, is transmitted solely through sex—vaginal, oral, or anal. Young women and teenage girls are the most susceptible to being infected by the chlamydia bacteria.

The Symptoms

Unfortunately, symptoms are often so mild, most women who contract chlamydia don't know they have the disease, which is why it's important to consult with your doctor or health professional to determine if a test should be considered. Women who do display symptoms usually notice them one to three weeks after being infected. Those signs include one or more of the following: abnormal vaginal discharge, burning when urinating, lower back pain or lower abdominal pain, nausea, fever, bleeding other than during menstruation, and pain during intercourse.

The Complications
Common as it is, if not treated, chlamydia can lead to very serious problems, both early in the disease and in its later stages. These complications include pelvic inflammatory disease (PID), which can cause lasting damage to a woman's fallopian tubes, uterus, as well as the surrounding tissue. In rare cases, a woman can die from an ectopic pregnancy caused, initially, by chlamydia. This is, as we said, a potentially very serious STD.

The Treatment
The good news is that chlamydia can be treated and cured with a single or week-long dose of antibiotics. As with each of the STDs discussed here, completely abstain from sex with your partner until you know you have not contracted the disease or that both of you are completely cured. (In the case of HIV, which we will discuss, there is no cure; but safe sex is still possible.)

Genital Herpes
You no doubt know someone with genital herpes or have seen ads for products to treat this STD. In fact, you might have contracted the disease earlier in life, as tens of millions of people across the country have this common STD. But if you have never had a symptom and you suddenly do display the symptoms of the disease, then the odds are you recently contracted the disease from your husband. Though female-to-male transmission is not nearly as likely as male to female, the sudden

appearance of the disease means that your husband has infected you. The only other option—an unlikely but plausible one—is the chance that you or he were infected years earlier, didn't notice the early symptoms, and the disease has lain dormant for years only to reappear now.

The Symptoms

It's usually during the very first outbreak of genital herpes that the symptoms are the most obvious—blisters in or around the genital area that break, turning into tender ulcers that take a few weeks to heal. In fact, there are two kinds of genital herpes, one causing blisters in the genital area and the other causes blisters similar to fever blisters on the mouth and lips. The first outbreak can also be accompanied by fever, swollen glands, and even a second outbreak.

The Complications

At its worst, genital herpes can reoccur on an infrequent basis, bringing with it the painful sores. Many doctors note that the anxiety associated with worrying if an outbreak will reoccur is another consequence of having the disease.

The Treatment

The disease, which can be diagnosed by a health care professional as well as by lab tests, is not curable, but it is highly treatable with antiviral medication. Doctors frequently recommend taking medication on a daily basis to suppress the disease and the likelihood of transmitting it. And, of course, immediately stop having sex with your partner, for if he is the source he can easily infect you again.

Genital Human Papillomavirus (HPV)

Though genital HPV is the most common STD, it's also the one that most people who are infected have no idea they have (or once had). In most cases, our own bodies fight off the disease, returning infected cells back to normal. But in a small minority of cases, genital HPV can turn into genital warts, which are not dangerous, or it can turn into cervical cancer, which is very serious. As with genital herpes, you or your spouse might have been infected years earlier, so if you do discover that you have genital HPV, there is no absolute certainty that you got it recently from your husband (who got it from his lover). In fact, about half of all sexually active women and men acquire genital HPV sometime in their lives.

The Symptoms and Complications

The most common symptom is the appearance of genital warts, though only about one in one hundred infected people get them. The warts appear as small bumps in the genital area. If it is a new infection, it will occur weeks or months after exposure. The warts will not become cancerous, but the disease can lead to cervical cancer, which is why it's vital to be screened for cervical cancer.

The Treatment

Your best treatment is yourself, as your own immune system is usually able to fight off the genital HPV infection. If you do develop clearly visible warts, medication can remove them, though the warts usually disappear all by themselves. The far more dangerous consequence, of course, is cervical cancer, which is why routine Pap testing is vital.

Gonorrhea

This common—and potentially dangerous—bacterial infection is one of the easiest to spread of all the STDs. Worse, gonorrhea does not always produce symptoms in men or women, making transmission even more likely, as some carriers have no idea they have it.

The Symptoms

While some victims—women and men—have no symptoms at all, even those who are symptomatic don't feel anything's wrong, as the clues are often mild or can easily be confused with an infection of the bladder or vagina. In women, these symptoms might be some burning when urinating and vaginal bleeding or discharge. Men too could experience burning when urinating, a discharge, abscesses and testicular swelling.

The Complications

Even though the symptoms of gonorrhea can be deceptively mild, the complications of the disease can be dire. In women it can lead to pelvic inflammatory disease (PID), which in advanced stages can cause chronic pelvic pain, damage to the fallopian tubes, and even life-threatening ectopic pregnancy. It can also cause severe damage to the blood and joints. This is a *very* serious STD if untreated.

The Treatment

A number of highly effective antibiotics completely cure gonorrhea, though the drugs can't reverse the damage this dangerous STD can wreak on a body. It's important that if you have any pain urinating, a discharge, or sore, seek medical advice immediately. And just as quickly, stop having sex with your partner who might have given you this STD.

Trichomoniasis

While young women are the most common victims of this STD, women and men of any age are susceptible. It's caused by a parasite that usually infects the vagina. In men the infection is usually in the urinary canal.

The Symptoms

Most often, men have no symptoms at all, which makes the

transmission of the disease all the more likely, as the man has no idea he's carrying the trichomoniasis infection. With women it's a different story, as the symptoms, which can begin to occur five to twenty-eight days after exposure, are obvious and painful. These include a vaginal discharge and pain when urinating or pain during intercourse.

The Complications
The pain and unpleasant discharge caused by the disease are its most serious consequences, although as with most STDs, it also increases susceptibility to HIV infection if a woman is exposed to that virus.

The Treatment
This is another easily treatable STD, as it usually can be completely cured with a single dose of a prescription medication. The problem is that since the man usually has no idea he has it because it's basically symptom-free for men, he can easily reinfect a woman (all the more reason to immediately stop having sex with your husband if you've been diagnosed).

Syphilis
The two main problems with syphilis is that first, in its early stage, the chief symptom is usually a sore that disappears on its own, which allows the disease to get progressively worse the longer it remains untreated; second, in the secondary stage, a rash may appear and also vanish even when untreated. And then the disease is able to survive, often for many years with no signs at all. But all the while, severe damage is being done to the heart, brain, liver, blood vessels, bones, and joints. Blindness, dementia, and paralysis are the final consequences of this insidious disease.

The Symptoms

In the first stage, usually ten days to three months after infection, a small, round, firm, single sore may appear (or there could be multiple sores). If you experience this symptom, immediately seek medical advice and stop having sex. The sore will disappear on its own, but the infection progresses to its second stage. Here's where the rashes appear, usually on the palms of the hands or the bottom of the feet. Other secondary symptoms include fever and swollen glands, which also vanish without a trace and without treatment. But the disease lingers on, slowly, steadily, and stealthily causing great damage. Other than HIV, this is the most dangerous STD to contract.

Treatment

If there's good news associated with syphilis, it's this: In the very first stage when the sore appears a single shot of penicillin or other antibiotics completely cures the disease. If you suspect your husband has been cheating, and you have anything that resembles early-stage symptoms, it's vital that you seek the advice of a medical professional. And your husband should too. But if you don't treat the disease in its early stages, it can stay in the body for years and eventually cause great harm.

HIV

And finally HIV, the infamous infection that ultimately can lead to full-blown AIDS. We certainly don't want to appear overly dramatic by including HIV and AIDS in this list of STDs a cheating spouse can bring home. And in fact, the chances of your contracting even the least harmful of the STDs are, we hope, slim. But they are not nil, and the consequences of infection are too important to overlook. That includes HIV, the slow but deadly disease that progresses steadily, coursing throughout the body. It's the first stage of the disease we want to focus on here, as signs do occur early, and proper diagnosis can be extremely advantageous to someone who's contracted the disease.

The Symptoms

Early-stage symptoms of HIV occur a few weeks after the disease has been contracted. These symptoms, lasting a few weeks before they disappear, are typically flulike or resemble the symptoms of mononucleosis. If you have such symptoms and believe your husband is sleeping with another person, it would be prudent to consult with a medical professional to see if you should be tested for HIV. In any event, these symptoms disappear, and you then might not have any other symptoms for years or even a decade (which is the second stage). But then the third stage arrives with full-blown AIDS, which you know is a debilitating, deadly disease.

Again, the likelihood of his being infected with HIV and infecting you is remote—but HIV and the other STDs are diseases that can have serious health consequences. You can't be too careful, especially if you're dealing with a careless cheater.

The Other Extreme Sign: Spousal Abuse

As if cheating weren't hurtful enough, far too often we see clients who also suffer from the indignity—or worse—of spousal abuse. Of course a spouse who emotionally, sexually, economically, or physically abuses his partner might not be having an affair. They don't go hand in hand in every case or even in the majority of cases. But in our experience, an abusive husband is a prime candidate for being an adulterous husband as well.

The reason a man inflicts one or more forms of abuse on his wife lies deep within his twisted psyche. But experts we've consulted with over the years to help our clients deal with all forms of spousal abuse say that at its core, abuse is used to control the wife, to make her feel and act totally subjugated and dependent upon the husband. But when that husband is having an affair, the abuse can become magnified, as the husband feels even more internal demands to have control over his wife. We therefore always regard spousal abuse as a possible warning sign of a husband's cheating. At the very least, if your husband is displaying obvious signs of spousal abuse and is not cheating on you, it is still important that you take immediate and positive action to protect yourself and your children from the horrendous effects that such dismal and debilitating treatment can inflict. The four types of spousal abuse are psychological, sexual, economic, and physical.

The Power of Words

The most common form of abuse a man inflicts upon his wife or partner is not attacking her with his hands but using words and actions to psychologically torment her. The "but stones will never hurt me" part of the old adage doesn't work here. In fact, name-calling, outbursts of screaming, accusations leveled in private and in public to humiliate are all common, powerful tactics used by abusers. No matter what the insult or charge is, the goal, usually achieved, is to degrade and eventually devastate a woman's self-image. Even *not* speaking to her at all is an effective form of passive-aggressive psychological abuse.

When a husband's accusations seem to focus on his wife's flirting with other men, or if he brings up in disparaging ways previous relationships she's had, this could be a sign that he's having an affair or at least desires one. Also, when this form of abuse seems to be getting worse, turns more intense, or occurs more frequently, there's a possibility that his guilt over having an affair is exacerbating the already intolerable psychological abuse he levies upon his wife. Suffering this or any form of abuse is not acceptable and can be life threatening. Any person in this situation must immediately seek help (see p. 176 for suggestions).

When Love Has Nothing to Do with Lovemaking

Your marriage doesn't entitle your husband to have forced sex with you. If your husband demands that you engage in sex when you don't want to, or if he forces you to participate in what you feel are demeaning sexual acts, then you're a victim of sexual abuse, married or not. A sexually abusive husband who is having sex outside marriage might be venting his frustrations and guilt by accusing his wife of cheating and uses forced sex as a way to punish her. If you suspect—or know—your husband is having an affair and he has a history of being abusive, sexually abusing you could be a component of his having an affair. In any event, no one should be forced to have unwanted sex. If you find yourself in this position, immediately seek help (see p. 176 for suggestions).

The Cost of Economic Abuse

Though likely never articulated by an abusive husband, the hidden purpose behind every act of his spousal abuse is complete control and mastery over the wife. By having command of the finances, an abusive husband is able to regulate much of what his wife can and cannot do outside of his purview.

Your husband is economically abusing you if he doles out an allowance, demands a full and detailed accounting of every penny you spend, threatens to cut you off financially, or even dictates that you take only the kind of job he feels you should have.

Controlling your finances to the point of making you totally dependent gives him the added benefit of keeping you from seeing how he's spending his own money, which could be on an affair. If this paralyzing economic abuse has reached a point where you have no life of your own, it's time to get help (see p. 176 for suggestions).

When Abuse Gets Physical

As harsh as psychological, sexual, and economic abuse are, the most dangerous form of spousal abuse is domestic violence; that is, using the fists to hit or slap, kicking, throwing or smashing objects, choking, and using or threatening to use a weapon. If you are ever treated in this way, even only once, by your husband, you can receive protection from the police, protection that could save your life.

Obviously, all men who cheat don't beat and abuse their wives, and all men who are physical abusers aren't necessarily cheaters. But a man who has little compulsion about physically harming his own wife obviously has scant regard for the mutual respect inherent in the marriage contract. And we've seen too many cases where the cheated-on wife has been a victim of physical and other abuse at some time in her marriage. Whether adultery is real or suspected in such a marriage, you need to extricate yourself from harm's way and seek help for yourself and your children (see p. 176 for suggestions).

Address the Abuse before the Adultery

First, deal with the reality that you're living with an abuser. Grappling with the suspicion that he's also likely a cheater comes next. Adultery is extremely harmful, hurtful, and can shake a marriage to its core. Abuse can be even more damaging, as it can actually endanger your well-being, health, and life. If abuse in any of the forms we've discussed is present in your marriage at levels that make your life intolerable and unbearable (only you can be the judge of that), your focus needs to be on ending the abuse now and forever. This likely means taking yourself out of the situation, away from the source of the abuse. While we deal with helping women find out if their spouse is cheating, whenever we see evidence of abuse we strongly advise our clients to first deal with their own safety and only then worry about catching the cheater. And we advise you to do the same. If you consider yourself to be in an abusive relationship, you need to seek help now. Stopping the abuse has to take priority over dealing with a suspected or proven affair. We and Dr. Gunzburg strongly advise you to get the help you need—be it legal, law enforcement, therapy, or all of these avenues of help. The following organizations offer immediate help and advice:

- National Domestic Violence/Child Abuse/Sexual Abuse: 800-799-SAFE (7233)/800-787-3224
- Domestic Violence Hotline: 800-829-1122
- Abuse Victim Hotline (free legal counsel and advice for victims of abuse): 877-448-8678

Turning to Dr. Gunzburg: How to Find Love and Respect for the Person Who Needs It Most

Surviving an affair, or worse, surviving one in which abuse has occurred, can be devastating to your self-image, sapping you of the love and respect you should have for yourself, the love and respect you deserve to feel about yourself as a person. Right now, you might believe that you'll never again have the capacity to feel any sense of respect or admiration for yourself. You might feel as if you've been trampled upon so thoroughly that you can't envision yourself as a successful and happy person, someone who can look at herself in the mirror and say, "I like and admire that person." Let me assure you that you not only have the capacity to become that person, but that you *will* become that person. It doesn't take a miracle, but it does take work. And that work can begin here.

Step One: Take Personal Responsibility for Your Life

I know, taking responsibility for your life sounds like a gargantuan and most improbable task right now. But it's much more within your grasp than you realize. First, recognize that you are the one person—the only person—who is responsible for your own life. Your partner isn't. Your parents, relatives, and closest friends aren't responsible for your life—only *you* are. You might ask, "What? I am responsible for the way I've been treated and the cause of the affair?" Of course not. The way you've been treated and the affair are not your fault. What I mean by taking responsibility is that you have responsibility for the actions you decide to take, actions that directly affect the kind of life you want to live.

Giving yourself the power and the authority to do what you truly want to do with your life—*that* is taking responsibility. No one else in the world is you, no one else has the ability to live the life that only you can live. And of course it follows that only you can fully and personally experience the results, good and less than good, derived directly from the decisions you made and the actions you took. Yes, people around you are affected in lesser and greater degrees by the consequences of your decisions and actions. But you more than anyone will benefit from and can be harmed by the ramifications of your choices, which is all the more reason to make your decisions your own. Take responsibility for them. It's your life. Live it.

A key to the success of living your own life is appreciating the fact that all along the way the choices themselves are not what matters most. How you handle your choices is what counts, including those choices that might have led to a great disappointment or failure. In every bad choice or unfortunate decision you can always find a nugget or even an entire vein of value. Doing that, taking what was worthwhile and valuable even in a failure, enables you to use that episode constructively later in life. Making a mistake then can be seen in a positive light, as a way of growing, of understanding yourself better. As you recognize that your life *is* your life and only you are allowed to be responsible for it, you will gain a sense of self-worth and even empowerment that will help you to live your life the way you want to live it.

Step Two: Get Real

When you take responsibility for your life, it doesn't mean that you'll take control of the universe and make everything just the way you'd like it to be. The affair has shown you that this isn't possible. But you still need to run a continual reality check here, putting things in perspective, appreciating what you can and what you cannot do. Recognize and relish your strengths and don't curse your weaknesses. Put all your qualities, all aspects of who you are, all your strengths and all your weaknesses in perspective. By applying this reality check, you actually gain even more control over living your life the way you want to. For you'll know how to use your strengths and how to work around your weaknesses.

Step Three: Have a Good Time

Yes, you read right. As important as building your self-respect and love for yourself is, it should not be regarded as a somber task. It's far easier to like yourself more when you're having a good time doing it. Of course, right now you're experiencing a terrible and terrifyingly stressful situation. But this doesn't mean you have lost all capacity to enjoy those things that have always been satisfying and pleasant experiences—getting lost in a historical novel, spending the day in the garden, renting *It's a Mad, Mad, Mad, Mad World* and laughing for two hours straight. If you came to my office as a client, I would ask you to write down four or five things that you love to do. Then I would ask you to do them one by one. When you have done everything on the list, have a personal awards ceremony of sorts, giving yourself the "Had A Great Time Achievement Award." This might sound silly, and perhaps that's the point: You'll have a good time doing this. It's your life, and you more than anyone deserves to enjoy it, even in times like these.

Step Four: Remember, You Are No Stranger to Success
No, I don't know you, but I do know that you've had your share of true successes in the past, and each and every one of them can help you achieve the self-admiration and self-respect you deserve in the future. You can call upon, conjure up as it were, these past successes with the goal of using what those earlier achievements felt like to help you see that you are capable of successes in the future. First, you need to recall some previous successes, and that's actually easier than you might imagine. If you came to my office as a client, I would ask you to write down a list of earlier successes—from childhood, an academic achievement, sporting events, large holiday parties that came off without a hitch, awards at work, whatever. Then relax in a comfortable chair, close your eyes, breathe deeply, and let your mind wander. When you feel you're in a comfortable state, recall a previous success and relive it, feel it, and deeply experience it, grabbing on to that feeling of success. Once done, slowly release the memory, open your eyes, and even though you'll be back in the present, you'll bring back with you that sense of success and self-worth. The result is a strengthening

of your confidence, which is precisely what you need at times like these.

Step Five: See a Future of Successes

When someone is going through what you are, the present and the future can appear the same: bleak. In fact, some people imagine their future as being even worse than their life today. They do that as a way of girding themselves for such a fate: If I think it'll be really bad, maybe it won't be. The ploy only succeeds in perpetuating negativity and a more depressing outlook. Viewing the future in such negative ways certainly is understandable at a time like this. But it can be harmful to recovery. Here's why: First, no one, including yourself, knows how the future is going to play out. When you think that the future is going to hold only more of the same problems and unhappiness or worse, the effect is to make today feel terrible at best. Second, if you truly and intensely believe that the future is going to be awful, you are more inclined to do negative things that can actually contribute to and help shape your low expectations and depressing scenario of the future.

So rather than putting your energies into such a hopeless future, picture one filled with success and happier times. And I do mean picture it, following the same technique I described in step four. This time, however, when you recall a previous success, also look ahead into your future and transfer that feeling of success from the past into the future. See yourself in that future, and at the same time surround the image with the feeling of success. Then, as in step four, bring yourself back to the present. Sure, the technique might sound a little otherworldly, but it's an excellent tool to use to help lessen negative thinking while increasing your sense of self-worth, which is critically important right now—and always.

Step Six: See Failure in a Different Light

Everybody makes mistakes and suffers from unpleasant incidents. And every mistake, catastrophe, and upheaval can be seen in two ways—always thoroughly negative or as something to learn from, to grow from. Only the latter approach of looking at failure and upsetting episodes as an opportunity for growth can help to reshape your life in positive ways. If you don't take the positive approach, every disappointment becomes a larger failure in your eyes, another reason to feel bad about yourself. But if you see negative events as opportunities for growth rather than as more reasons to accept life as just a string of failures, you'll gain control over moving your life forward.

Step Seven: Take Charge

Action matters. How you act defines who you are, as the actions we take have a profound effect on how we feel and how we think. For example, taking bold action helps to build self-confidence. I'm not suggesting that you act recklessly, but don't shy away from taking strong, definitive action, as each positive action you take ratchets up your self-confidence level. The action and the feeling of confidence are intrinsically linked. Especially at this stage, you need to have the confidence and assurance to move ahead. So be prepared to take charge—your self-worth will be very glad you did.

By taking these steps, not everything in the world will be right again. But you will begin to respect and like, even love, the person who most needs that from you: yourself.

CHAPTER 9
And in the End . . .

. . . the love you take is equal to the love you make.
—*The Beatles*

By any measure, matrimonial private investigation is not your typical profession. We're hired as sleuths, but in the process of providing that service we also become our client's confidant, adviser, shoulder to lean on and to cry on, and perhaps most of all, her friend. And though we've never met you, we hope that in our having guided you through the panoply of ways to discern, catalog, and act upon the warning signs of a cheating spouse, you have come to regard us as your friends as well.

Because we know what you've probably been through these past weeks or months—the stresses, the fears, the anger, and the sense of loss—we feel as if we do know you. And we sincerely wish you the very best of luck in resolving what has to be one of the greatest crises of your life. It's a crisis that bursts out into the open when you finally confront your husband with the evidence you've gathered through applying the knowledge, techniques, and advice that we have gained in our decades of helping people who were in the same place you are now. And it all reaches a culmination when you finally confront your spouse with the evidence. When do you know it's the right time to do this? As we said at the beginning of *Warning Signs*, there is a moment many of our clients experience, a moment when they hear themselves saying, "Enough!" By now, having learned so much, and having gathered and documented the evidence of his cheating, you probably have reached your "Enough!" moment, as your proof is not just compelling but overwhelmingly convincing. If the time is now, if you've reached your "Enough!" moment, but are unsure how to turn your proof into action, we are here to give you our final suggestions, ones that show you how to confidently and constructively confront him with the charge of being a cheater.

Each of these suggestions is designed to help you confront your partner in ways that work to put *you* in charge, so you will no longer be a victim. The suggestions will also help to enhance the prospects of your reconciling, if that is indeed what the two of you determine is best. In fact, most couples can indeed survive an affair. And to that end, we recommend that you visit Dr. Gunzburg's website, www.healing-marriage-infidelity.com, to learn how you and your partner can survive infidelity and build a stronger, healthier, and happier relationship. But right now you need to focus on confronting the cheater with the fact that you know. Here, then, are suggestions on how to handle the culmination of all you've learned: telling your partner that you know he's been cheating on you.

Proof positive
- As we've said throughout *Warning Signs*, do not act prematurely or in haste—make sure you have assembled ample, overwhelmingly incontrovertible proof that cheating has occurred—whether it's three condoms in the bottom of his briefcase, unambiguous text messages and emails from and to his lover, receipts from hotels and restaurants, or a combination of other major signs we've taught you to look for. So confront him only if and when you have all the proof you feel you need, which you probably do have by now.

Keep it private
- When you do confront him, do it in complete privacy. No relatives, no friends, and certainly no children. This is between you and your partner and no one else. Have

someone present only if you are truly and realistically worried about your or his safety once the truth is out.

Here's the story
- Tell him this is going to be the most serious talk you've ever had with him, and you want his complete attention, respect, and honesty. Then tell him you know he's cheating, and here is the proof. Then lay it out, preferably in one sentence, which you've composed beforehand. "I found three condoms in your briefcase last month, I have receipts from five hotels where you stayed with her, and here's her cell phone number." And no more, no editorializing, just let the impact of the proof show him the truth is out. You should know that some infidelity experts advise against telling the cheater what the precise evidence is, for they worry he can use the information to better conceal his affairs in the future. But it's our experience that piling on the evidence quickly and completely is more effective at undermining his excuses and any attempt at a defensive rebuttal.

Expect Vesuvius, or not
- When you tell him, there will likely be an eruption of emotion, with his yelling that none of it is true; or you might experience just the opposite reaction, utter silence, as his defenses will make him freeze and become literally speechless. But you'll be better off to be prepared for the explosion of emotion. You might hear him deny it all completely and try to flip the confrontation around, saying that it's all in your imagination or worse. Don't stand for that, tell him you have the facts and he's cheating and now let's discuss it. You must stay in control of the confrontation conversation, so do not allow him to start talking about you. You are there to talk about the fact that he's cheated. Period.

Have tissues at hand
• Not necessarily for you but for him. Be prepared for
another kind of outburst—crying. *His* crying. If that
occurs, remain tough, do not try to console or comfort
him. You don't need to denigrate him either; just let
him cry. He brought this on himself, and the crying can
serve as a kind of catharsis for him, though a temporary one. Again: Do not let his tears soften your resolve
to confront him fully and completely.

Remember at all times: He can be really *sneaky*
• Cheaters can be very clever, as you've seen in *Warning
Signs*, and when confronted some will coolly say there's
simply no way I could have cheated, as I just love you
and the kids so much. Don't allow his faux sincerity to
deflect you or give you pause. You *know* he's cheating,
and his denials are just a cynical continuation of it.

Two steps forward, one back
• Once the confrontation conversation settles down, after
the shock of your telling him that you know the truth,
discuss next steps. The first step that we suggest is that
you see a counselor and/or seek help from other reliable
sources, and there are many. As we mentioned, Dr. Gunzburg offers a highly regarded program on his website
for couples who want to survive the affair; our own
website, www.infidelity.com, provides advice, support,
and discussion boards for individuals and couples who
have been affected by infidelity. And there are many
other resources available to you online and in your community. If possible, find a professional, accredited counselor who specializes in marriage and relationships. We
particularly caution you against relying solely or primarily on your immediate family and close friends for
advice, for as loving and concerned as they are, they are

not equipped to give you the kind of objective, informed, and therapeutic advice that a professional can provide at this most critical juncture.

This does not mean the end
• And finally, as horrific as the revelation of an affair can be, and it *will* be awful, it does not spell the absolute end of your relationship. The end is not at hand, not if you two don't want it to be. The affair can actually play a transformative role in making your relationship stronger, more honest, and more rewarding to each of you individually and to you as a couple.

So no, an affair does not have to be the end, but we are very grateful to be able to play a role in bringing the affair to an end. We wish you the best and would love to hear from you. Please email us at tonyanddawn@infidelity.com.

Internet Resources

Using the Internet as a resource for information, help, guidance and support.

We created www.infidelity.com to help people like you deal with every stage of infidelity, from suspecting it, to discovery, clear through to recovery. If you visit www.infidelity.com, please be sure to stop by our discussion boards, as there you'll find an entire community of people who've been affected by infidelity—their insights and support can prove to be invaluable for you. Also, Dr. Gunzburg's own website, howtosurviveanaffair .com, can also be of great benefit to you.

Listed here, alphabetically, are other excellent online resources for people who suspect infidelity, or are searching for information on how to deal with it. We've divided these online resources into two main groups: the first deals primarily with catching a cheating partner; the second lists resources focusing on saving a relationship that's been affected by infidelity, or, if you feel divorce is your only option, how to best handle that solution.

Of course, these are only a tiny fraction of the ever-growing number of websites that offer help for individuals and couples whose lives have been affected by infidelity—so we encourage you to explore the Web for resources. As you'll see, there is a world of help awaiting you.

Websites offering help, information and relevant products and services to those who suspect infidelity is a part of their relationship

catch-a-cheating-wife.com

> A commercial website selling spyware and similar items to help individuals catch a cheating wife or husband.

chatcheaters.com

> A comprehensive website offering articles, products, books and forums for individuals who are going through the various stages of infidelity, from suspicion to full recovery.

cheating-spouse-guide.com

> A commercial website offering a free guide, and sells spyware and similar items to help individuals catch a cheating wife or husband.

cheatingspousepi.com

> A commercial private investigational website offering access to private investigators; the site also includes articles on cheating spouses.

cyber-cheaters.com

> A commercial website which sells spyware to catch a wife or husband who is suspected of engaging in cyber-sex or of having an affair.

cyberwidows.tripod.com

> As this support website states: "Our goal is to give the betrayed an arena to make some sort of sense of what has happened to him/her, steps to take toward healing, and a sense that you are not alone."

emailrevealer.com

> A commercial website which offers a wide variety of email searches, including finding if a spouse is using an online dating service, identification of a person by an email address, plus phone searches, background checks and similar identification services.

infidelity.com

> The Internet's largest informational, support and community website dedicated to helping individuals at every stage of infidelity, from discovery to recovery with articles, discussion boards, forums and support services; the site was founded by Tony DeLorenzo and Dawn Ricci.

infidelityadvice.com

> An informational and commercial website offering articles and advice about infidelity; the site also offers a book on catching a cheating spouse.

infidelitycheck.org

> A basic, commercial website selling a variety of spyware and similar items to help individuals catch a cheating wife or husband.

infidelityhelp.com

> An informational and professional services website featuring Dr. Don-David Lusterman, a clinical psychologist; the site offers his books as well as information on infidelity.

infidelity-help.us.com

> An informational and commercial website offering articles about infidelity as well as products to help an individual catch a cheating spouse.

94truth.com

> A commercial website for individuals seeking the assistance of a professional private investigator anywhere in the country; the site also provides a directory of matrimonial attorneys. (This is the site for our matrimonial private investigation agency.)

truthaboutdeception.com

> An informational website dealing with lying, infidelity, love and romance; the site is the effort of "a group of scholars, scientists, and working professions interested in sharing information about why people lie to, and cheat on, those they love."

spygear4u.com

> A commercial website offering an extensive selection of spyware and similar items to help individuals catch a cheating wife or husband.

slimtrakgps.com

> A commercial website offering a line of GPS tracking products used by individuals to track a cheating spouse.

thespydirectory.com

> A basic commercial directory website listing a handful of links to companies offering spyware and other related products.

trac-pro.com

> A commercial website offering a line of GPS tracking products used for a variety of needs, including tracking a cheating spouse.

suicidepreventionlifeline.org

A suicide prevention lifeline website. "From immediate suicidal crisis to information about mental health, crisis centers in our network are equipped to take a wide range of calls." The "lifeline" number is 1-800-273-TALK.

Websites offering help to individuals and couples who are dealing with infidelity and those who are ready to move beyond it

acenterformarriagecounseling.com

A therapist's professional website detailing couples counseling and marriage counseling in the Philadelphia, PA, area; the site, and practice, belongs to Arlene Foreman, M.S.

affairs-help.com

A therapist's professional website featuring Emily M. Brown, LCSW, Director of Key Bridge Therapy and Mediation Center in Arlington, VA.

afterinfidelity.com

A therapist's professional website featuring Judith Barnett, marriage counselor, who specializes in infidelity and affair counseling in Chapel Hill, NC.

aftertheaffair.net

An informational and commercial website featuring Katie Coston and her book "Infidelity Crisis: How to Gain Forgiveness and Respect After Your Affair."

askmaple.com

> An informational website with a focus on surviving infidelity; besides articles and links to resources, the site also offers books on the topic.

beyondaffairs.com

> An informational and resource website "dedicated to helping couples prevent affairs, and providing specialized help for couples and individuals recovering from affairs." It is operated by Anne and Brian Bercht, who are authors, speakers, and relationship coaches.

break-free-from-the-affair.com

> A comprehensive informational infidelity website featuring Dr. Robert Huizenga; his books and his lessons are available for download.

broken-heart-help.com

> An informational and commercial website that provides "resources to the broken hearted, to help you get through the hard times, despite how impossible it can feel." The site features articles and books for sale.

dearpeggy.com

> One of the oldest and still one of the most comprehensive and useful websites for any person or couple having to deal with infidelity. The site and its founder, Peggy Vaughan, offer articles, books, counseling, access to support groups, and numerous helpful resource links.

divorce360.com

> An informational and useful website that "provides help, advice and community for people contemplating, going through or recovering from divorce and the issues around it—custody, child support, alimony and litigation."

divorcebusting.com

An professional website featuring Michele Weiner-Davis, M.S.W., an author and marriage therapist who "believes that the vast majority of divorces...are absolutely unnecessary because most relationship problems are solvable." Her books are sold on the website.

divorcecentral.com

An informational, resource and support website which provides "the opportunity to communicate with others who are in various stages of decision-making, mourning, mediating, settling, litigating, and just plain 'dealing.'"

divorcemagazine.com

A divorce and separation resource website providing information and advice about divorce law, divorce lawyers, family law, children and divorce, and other divorce-related issues, as well as information on family lawyers and online divorce.

divorcenet.com

A divorce and separation resource website offering state-specific articles, an online community and a nationwide directory of divorce lawyers, mediators and financial professionals.

divorcesource.com

A resource website for vital divorce related information; it also carries a supportive atmosphere through its interactive support community and its chat rooms as well as its large network of professionals who are accessible through its professional directory.

divorcesupport.com

> A divorce support website that provides divorce information on family law topics such as divorce, child custody, visitation, child support, alimony and property division.

divorcetransitions.com

> A divorce information website for those anticipating, experiencing, or recovering from separation and divorce. It includes lists of book and booklets, articles, resources, as well as ask-the-experts columns.

drbalternatives.com

> The professional website of Donna R. Bellafiore, MSW, LCSW, with over 20 years experience specializing in individual and couples counseling, including infidelity issues and divorce mediation.

encouragementinstitute.com

> The professional website of Katherine Ann Best, Ph.D., LCSW, the founder of the Encouragement Institute, a licensed psychotherapist and professor at the University of South Florida.

healthyplace.com

> A consumer mental health website providing comprehensive information on psychological disorders and psychiatric medications from both a consumer and expert point of view.

howtosurviveanaffair.com

> The infidelity recovery informational and help website featuring Dr. Frank Gunzburg and his book, "How to Survive An Affair, Saving Your Marriage and How to

Forgive and Work Through the Past." Dr. Gunzburg contributed to the writing of "Warning Signs."

imagotherapy.com

Website for a nonprofit organization whose mission is to transform the world one relationship at a time and create a new model for marriage. More than 1,900 therapists practice Imago Therapy in more than 20 countries.

judithbarnett.com

The professional website for Judith S. Barnett, Ph.D., a licensed clinical psychologist, located in Chapel Hill, NC, who has helped individuals and couples for over 20 years. She is a certified Imago Relationship Therapist and Marriage Counselor.

loveletterbox.com

A community website that offers support to persons seeking relationship advice with problems or questions regarding love issues.

makeuporbreakupcounseling.com

A website that helps you discover how you can turn your relationship around—and possibly prevent a breakup. It offers couples articles, information and specialized programs.

marriageadvice.com

A website that offers a community of husbands and wives and who are working to create happy marriages that last a lifetime.

marriage-success-secrets.com

> A website that offers resources to help you determine if there is still hope for your marriage.

maximalhappiness.com

> Professional website of Dr. Rachna D. Jain, author, speaker, coach and psychologist who helps her clients live happier and more successful lives.

moderndatingsite.com

> A website providing dating tips and dating advice as well as free ebooks on romance and love.

passionatelife.ca

> A website for seminars dedicated to helping couples prevent affairs, and providing specialized help for couples and individuals recovering from affairs.

positive-way.com

> A website that offers help to couples, married or unmarried, single people looking for a relationship, and people wanting to improve their self-esteem and create more happiness in their lives.

relationshipgold.com

> A website offering love, relationship, and communication secrets for creating a lifetime of love. The founders of this site believe that life can be lived in a joyful, conscious, loving way.

relationship-institute.com

> A comprehensive relationship focused website offering relationship related programs, events, and articles. The philosophy of this site comes from a preventive/

educational approach to relationship creation and enhancement.

relationshipweb.com

A website offering first aid for relationships, with a directory of thousands of helpful relationship links, discussion forums, books, and help on affairs, marriage, dating, divorce, addiction, abuse, breakups, and more.

selfgrowth.com

A leading self improvement and personal growth website with over one million monthly visitors that offers inspirational quotes, event listings, articles, and more.

separateddads.co.uk

A website offering help and advice for separated fathers that was formed to offer a unique reference point on being away from or separated from your children. This site helps with ideas on how to cope when you are together or apart.

shirleyglass.com

A professional website for Shirley P. Glass, Ph.D., ABPP, an author and infidelity expert. The *New York Times* has referred to her as "the godmother of infidelity research."

singlerose.com

An emotionally supportive online publication for divorced, widowed and never married women raising children alone, offering articles by doctors, lawyers, psychologists and others on a topics of interest to single mothers.

singlespouse.com

> A website that offers support, fun and helpful resources. The community has an online dating service, chats and forums, as well as useful resources for getting support and financial assistance.

smartmarriages.com

> The website of the Coalition for Marriage, Family and Couples Education that is dedicated to making marriage education widely available. It provides couples with information to help create successful marriages.

stayinginlove.com

> The website from the authors of the book "From Sad to Glad: 7 Steps to Facing Change with Love and Power."

symcinc.com

> The website of Penny R Tupy, who offers marriage coaching and specializes in counseling those affected by infidelity, addiction, and abuse.

womansdivorce.com

> A website dedicated to helping women take control of their divorce; the website offers comprehensive information on the legal, financial, and emotional aspects, as well as articles for starting over.

worldclassmarriage.com

> A website from relationship experts Patty Howell and Ralph Jones (who have been married for over 25 years) who teach couples how to succeed in their relationships.

Calendars

Patterns of behavior are much easier to detect when you observe actions repeated on the same day or days of the week with some regularity. That's why we provide you with twelve day-to-day, month-by-month "Warning Signs" calendars here. We provide additional blank grid Calendars at the end of chapters 4, 5 and 7 to assist you in determining patterns in the behavior and actions detailed in each of those chapters.

Use these Calendars to detect anything else not covered in this book that seems strange or out of the ordinary to you, or for overflow information that you cannot fit into the grid calendars provided (for example, the email address of a potential lover, or the name of a restaurant where you saw them having a meal together.) There is one line for each day, and one page for each month. You can use these Calendars by themselves, or couple them with the grid Calendars for added space to write down your observances.

It might be easier for you to remove this and the other Calendars from "Warning Signs" so you can keep the Calendars in a folder where you're assembling other bits of proof, such as receipts. Or, of course, it lends itself quite easily to photocopying, which we encourage you to do.

JANUARY

1	
2	
3	
4	
5	
6	
7	
8	
9	
10	
11	
12	
13	
14	
15	
16	
17	
18	
19	
20	
21	
22	
23	
24	
25	
26	
27	
28	
29	
30	
31	

FEBRUARY

1	
2	
3	
4	
5	
6	
7	
8	
9	
10	
11	
12	
13	
14	
15	
16	
17	
18	
19	
20	
21	
22	
23	
24	
25	
26	
27	
28	
29	

MARCH

1	
2	
3	
4	
5	
6	
7	
8	
9	
10	
11	
12	
13	
14	
15	
16	
17	
18	
19	
20	
21	
22	
23	
24	
25	
26	
27	
28	
29	
30	
31	

APRIL

1	
2	
3	
4	
5	
6	
7	
8	
9	
10	
11	
12	
13	
14	
15	
16	
17	
18	
19	
20	
21	
22	
23	
24	
25	
26	
27	
28	
29	
30	

MAY

1	
2	
3	
4	
5	
6	
7	
8	
9	
10	
11	
12	
13	
14	
15	
16	
17	
18	
19	
20	
21	
22	
23	
24	
25	
26	
27	
28	
29	
30	
31	

JUNE

1	
2	
3	
4	
5	
6	
7	
8	
9	
10	
11	
12	
13	
14	
15	
16	
17	
18	
19	
20	
21	
22	
23	
24	
25	
26	
27	
28	
29	
30	

JULY

1	
2	
3	
4	
5	
6	
7	
8	
9	
10	
11	
12	
13	
14	
15	
16	
17	
18	
19	
20	
21	
22	
23	
24	
25	
26	
27	
28	
29	
30	
31	

AUGUST

1	
2	
3	
4	
5	
6	
7	
8	
9	
10	
11	
12	
13	
14	
15	
16	
17	
18	
19	
20	
21	
22	
23	
24	
25	
26	
27	
28	
29	
30	
31	

SEPTEMBER

1	
2	
3	
4	
5	
6	
7	
8	
9	
10	
11	
12	
13	
14	
15	
16	
17	
18	
19	
20	
21	
22	
23	
24	
25	
26	
27	
28	
29	
30	

OCTOBER

1	
2	
3	
4	
5	
6	
7	
8	
9	
10	
11	
12	
13	
14	
15	
16	
17	
18	
19	
20	
21	
22	
23	
24	
25	
26	
27	
28	
29	
30	
31	

NOVEMBER

1	
2	
3	
4	
5	
6	
7	
8	
9	
10	
11	
12	
13	
14	
15	
16	
17	
18	
19	
20	
21	
22	
23	
24	
25	
26	
27	
28	
29	
30	

DECEMBER

1	
2	
3	
4	
5	
6	
7	
8	
9	
10	
11	
12	
13	
14	
15	
16	
17	
18	
19	
20	
21	
22	
23	
24	
25	
26	
27	
28	
29	
30	
31	

Acknowledgments

We would like to give our deep thanks and appreciation to the following people whose guidance, support, and counsel have helped to make possible the creation of this book: our fabulous editor, Lara Asher, whose advice, patience, and encouragement will long be appreciated; our families who have always championed and nurtured us, but particularly so during the writing of this book, including Rocco and Geraldine DeLorenzo, Gina DeLorenzo, Anthony DeLorenzo Jr., Blair Baron, and Beatrice Lesser; and finally, and ultimately, the thousands of individual clients we've served and whose painful experiences we have called upon to help others find the truth.

Index

About the Authors

Together, **Tony DeLorenzo** and his wife **Dawn Ricci** have over 45 years experience as private investigators specializing in detecting and proving infidelity. Each has personally worked on thousands of cheating spouse cases.

Tony founded Allstate Investigations over 30 years ago, and within a few years grew the firm into one of the country's largest private detective agencies dedicated to matrimonial investigations—that is, to catching cheating spouses. In 2007, Dawn, with whom he had long shared administrative duties of the private investigations firm, became its president to enable Tony to develop www.infidelity.com. Today, www.infidelity.com is the internet's largest, most comprehensive, helpful, and trusted Website helping millions of individuals affected by infidelity and the emotional, health, financial, and social effects it causes.

Tony is among the most frequently called upon experts in the field of infidelity detection—having appeared on *Oprah Winfrey, The Today Show, 20/20,* CNN, *Tyra Banks, Inside Edition,* Fox, *Geraldo,* MSNBC, and dozens of other national television and radio shows.

A psychologist who has devoted himself to working with people in emotional pain, **Dr. Frank Gunzburg** has been in practice since 1975 helping couples and individuals survive trauma and heartbreak.

First licensed in 1975, Dr. Gunzburg earned his Ph.D. from American University in 1974, and prior to that earned an M.S. from Virginia Commonwealth University.

Visit Dr. Gunzburg's website at www.marriage-counselor-doctor.com for information about marriage, or www.healing-marriage-infidelity.com for infidelity. Dr. Gunzburg's published (eBook) programs include *Save Your Marriage and Stop Divorce* and *How to Survive an Affair*.

Ken Baron worked with Tony DeLorenzo in conceiving and developing www.infidelity.com where Ken is Senior Executive VP, Director of Content, and Member of the Board.